Getting amazing things done.™

in your crazy jammed life

™

What Successful Project Managers Know
and
How They Lead People to Do Amazing Things

HENRY LEWIS

This book was written to help you lead others and inspire them to do amazing, startling, wonderful things.

Here is a simple litmus test. Have you created an atmosphere that draws others to want to join the magic of your group, or do they want to escape from it? True leaders nurture an atmosphere in which teams thrive and grow and do great things. How's it going?

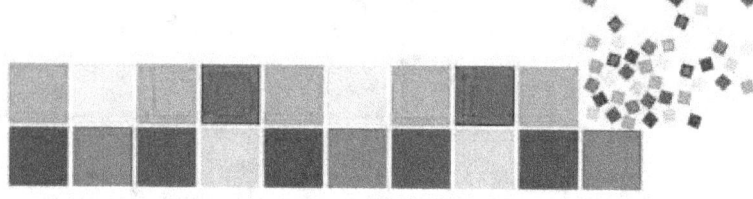

"Henry points out leadership principles to getting things done that result in amazing projects. For new and seasoned project managers, Henry highlights the impact of honesty, transparency, authenticity and care to build trust, to inspire them to be exceptional. 'Lead with grace and you will be rewarded beyond measure.'" *Thomas Walenta, PgMP, PMP, PMI Fellow - Germany*

"'Getting amazing things done' not just equips but inspires."
Ben Cox, Senior Director, Viewpoint Construction Software – US, Oregon

"Written in a friendly and engaging style… an important call to action for project managers to see themselves as leaders. Henry's experience and passion comes through with a challenge to think about what sort of leader we want to be and how we can improve our project outcomes."
Michael Coleman, PM Learning Program Manager, IBM - United Kingdom

"This book is truly amazing. A best read for all to understand project management."
Padmanabhan Venkataramanan, PMP, Leader PM Curriculum, IBM India (Retired) - India

"'Getting amazing things done' equips the aspiring Project Manager with every needed tool and then challenges her to remember the true key to success: the Team. How many leaders heap up knowledge but fail to inspire their people! You need to read it now."
Jancin Dick, PMP, former SVP Global Supply Chain, Pitney Bowes - US, New York

"Read and keep this book close to your hands. You will need it. For leaders of projects and organizations. I will use this book in my workshops of leading and project management."
Tadeu Veiga, PMP, Management and Professional Development Consultant, TadeuVR – Brazil

gettingamazingthingsdone.com

Cover design: Henry Lewis

Getting amazing things done™

in your crazy jammed life

What Successful Project Managers Know
and
How They Lead People to Do Amazing Things

HENRY LEWIS

"Getting amazing things done", "Getting amazing", and Getting amazing
logo are trademarks of Henry Lewis Consulting Inc.

"PMI", "PMP", and "PMBOK" are registered marks of Project Management Institute, Inc.

ISBN-13: 978-1-983-70372-0 (softcover)
ISBN-13: 978-0-692-09118-0 (Kindle)

Library of Congress Control Number: 2018903154

Credits for all citations are listed in back of the book under Bibliography
and Endnotes.

Published by Henry Lewis Consulting Inc
15602 Fairwood Lane, Minnetonka, Minnesota USA 55345

gettingamazingthingsdone.com

To Robbie,
Who lovingly encourages
me to dream.

*The first responsibility of a leader is to define
reality. The last is to say thank you.
In between the two, the leader must become a
servant and a debtor.*
Max DePree[i]

*What makes a good leader is that they eschew
the spotlight in favor of spending time and
energy to do what they need to do to support
and protect their people.*
Simon Sinek[ii]

Contents

Preface

A few words to kick this off. This book is my small attempt to convey the leadership principles that I have found so powerful in my years of leading teams of people to accomplish amazing things. Amazing things are not always what we expect them to be. Oftentimes *amazing* is expressed in meeting an unbelievable schedule or coming in substantially under budget. But not just that. It is doing so with the team intact and feeling good about the entire experience. It is reaching the finish line with a sense of true fulfillment on the part of every team member involved. True leaders *get it done*. They accomplish the project's mission and often much more. They do it in a way that fosters growth and excitement in everyone connected with the enterprise. Team members come away with a sense that they have been a part of something special, *something truly magnificent*. And they are right. But what is it that makes that possible? This book tries to answer that question.

If you are new to project management and want to know how to lead teams effectively, this book is for you. If you need a basic guidebook woven through with insights into achieving awesome results, this book will give you the tools to win and lead with deep passion. If you have been leading projects and teams for a while, and you long for *that special something* that will set your team apart and drive them to achieve stunning results, this book will unpack the secrets of leading well. These principles are what I have practiced on projects over the years and taught to thousands of others around the globe. They are principles that nurture extraordinary teams across time and culture, and they frequently deliver amazing, startling, wonderful results to the clients we serve.

However, if you are looking for a book to prepare you for the PMP® exam, this is not the book. It is not a prep course. I cover many of the core mechanics behind project management theory, but not exhaustively. I give you the basics that I have found are most essential to the success of projects and teams. These insights and tools are a framework for effectively leading teams of people working together on a common mission.

This book is about project management and the qualities of true leadership that are critical to winning. Blend these ideas with your own style and watch your teams exceed your expectations and, perhaps, even your dreams.

James Kouzes and Barry Posner hit it right on the mark in their classic book *Leadership Challenge*. They said,

> *Leaders speak to people's hearts and listen*
> *to their heartbeats because, in the final*
> *analysis, common caring is the way in which*
> *shared visions get enacted.*[iii]

My hope is that you will discover the joy of leading others as they accomplish goals that others thought were impossible.

Henry Lewis, Minnetonka, February 2018

Part 1

Introduction

Starting out

Ever found yourself working on a project or trying to accomplish a simple task, and the end of it just seemed to keep slipping through your fingers, slipping further into the future? Ever started an effort with a very clear understanding, and before too long a thousand other voices had changed the objective, and your purpose had become fuzzy and unclear? Have you ever thought you knew what was expected, only to find that others had a completely different idea of what you were supposed to do? These are all examples of how a task or set of tasks can go off the tracks, encounter numerous delays, and possibly never get done. These seem like simple to-dos. We are talking about a clearly understood objective, a specific mission. But often the *clearly understood* aspect vanishes in the light of day-to-day realities. So, do you like to get things done?

We are not boiling the ocean

This book is intended for those who just want to accomplish an objective. There is an old piece of business advice that says, "we are not boiling the ocean". It may seem a little quirky, but it makes an immediate point. Successful project management, or let's just say, successful *accomplishment of things* is rooted in a clear understanding of what we are called to do; what our mission is. Success in accomplishing tasks is grounded in a clear understanding of what we have been asked to do. By contrast, boiling the ocean refers to the classic problem of trying to do too much, trying to do everything, trying to do the impossible, with the limitations of what we have available. Believe it or not, most projects fail as they stumble on this single issue. We must have a clear definition of what we are here to accomplish. What is our mission? If we can get a grasp of the mission, if we can clearly acknowledge at the outset the boundaries of what we are doing, then we are already on the road to success. Let's begin.

Our mission

Who should read this book? First, of course, project managers. Whether you have the job title of project manager or not, many companies are assigning their people the job of "managing this or that project". What does that mean? How do you do that? Or maybe you have the title "project manager" after your name and you have struggled with success. Possibly you are launching a small company or running a department and wonder if you could use these principles. You can. Maybe you are in a leadership role and want to be more effective and lead well. This book can help.

Wherever you are, this book provides a road map for your success; tools and principles to guide you to successful achievement of your goals. Each chapter builds successively, laying out the basic principles of project management and leadership. I have made every effort to minimize technical jargon. I introduce terms, of course, but do not rely on them. I will lay out the basic principles of project management in language that people can understand and work with. This book is intended for aspiring leaders and project managers, seasoned professionals, and others in leadership positions at all levels.

But one more thing. Project management principles provide structure, but the principles alone will not accomplish our mission. We still need someone to lead the effort. This is where you come in.

Successful project managers are successful leaders. What is a successful leader? Throughout the book I have interspersed discussions that highlight important ideas about the nature of real leadership. These ideas will bring into focus critical leadership qualities that will help you lead successful projects and enrich your life and the lives of those you lead. With these principles and ideas in hand, accomplishing things and completing projects is within each of our grasp. There are no boundaries to the potential impact of your leadership on the lives of others and the success of your missions. Let me say that one more time – *there are no boundaries* to the potential impact of your leadership on the lives of others.

Stand back and get the big picture

Looking at the forest

So, on the one hand, we have our daily routine and cycle of life. But, on the other, we have special efforts or events that are outside the norm. And it is these special endeavors, these specific other tasks or groups of tasks we must do, that we call *projects*. These things that we try to accomplish *in addition to what we normally do* come with certain challenges. And often these additional things we wish to accomplish, we fail to ever get done.

When we initially stand back and consider what we want to accomplish through a project, we are often overwhelmed. The complexity is daunting and the expectations unrealistic. We cannot imagine where to begin. So, we just dive in, and often flounder, and sometimes we fail. Other times we think, "Ah, no big deal." We see the task as doable, and maybe we finish things more or less as we thought we would. But more often than not our *no big deal* projects unravel before us into an unending stream of things that never seems to end. Things seem to unravel to an infinite length. The forest is always there, but we must look at it with the eyes of a project manager. How does a project manager see the forest, or should we even be looking at all of these trees?

Beginning to define our world

As we consider what we have been asked to do, it can seem overwhelming. It can seem like looking at a dense forest. What is to be done? Let's begin by defining a few things.

A *project* is a specific objective with a defined start and end date, a defined goal intended to accomplish a tactical initiative over a relatively short-term time frame. There is intentionally some looseness in the definition. How specific is the objective? What delineates short-term? So, a project is designed to accomplish a specific goal within a defined, specific, short-term window of time. We get a better sense of this if we compare it to a program.

A *program* accomplishes a strategic mission over a long-range window of time. In fact, the purpose of a program may evolve over time. A program does not have a specific end date. It is launched and continues as long as the enterprise considers it useful in the overall strategy. Programs by their nature are often a compilation of projects. A program manager, for example, would provide oversight to numerous projects identified under some strategic initiative.

We should mention projects, and in some cases programs, are frequently managed within a broader organizational framework called a *project management office* (PMO). PMI® (Project Management Institute) defines a PMO as "An organizational structure that standardizes the project-related governance and facilitates the sharing of resources, methodologies, processes, tools, and techniques."[iv] Practically speaking, the PMO fosters a healthy project environment providing continuity in methodology, training, and structure by promoting industry accepted principles. This gives senior leadership a reliable and consistent view into the world of projects and how those projects are doing.

As we compare project and program, we see that a project focuses in on a discrete objective over a defined window of time. A program does neither of these. A project accomplishes tactical objectives, whereas a program meets strategic initiatives.

So, if you have specific things you want to accomplish in a specific period of time, you are talking about a project. Welcome to the party! Congratulations, now you are a project manager.

But you say to me, "I am still seeing the forest and not the individual trees. I am still feeling overwhelmed." Fair enough, I say, this is all quite normal. We will take this in steps, and we will unpack the mission of your project so that there is no apprehension or confusion.

We have a general understanding of what a project is. Now, what are the specifics of *your* project? Let's begin to get specific. It begins by agreeing to begin.

Begin by agreeing to begin

There is a certain daily rhythm in the life of an enterprise, just as there is a daily pulse in the atmosphere of any community. There is a pace of typical expectations and events in every area of our lives. These are not projects. They are just the ebb and flow of daily life in the organization. Projects are something else, something *in addition to* the regular things we do.

Projects are special events that are on top of or outside of the daily patterns of our days. Projects are defined by specific goals and boundaries. The *project charter* begins this definition. First, a project charter includes a high-level statement of the mission. This is not enough detail to begin the detailed work, but it sets the broad, initial boundary of our objective for the project. Second, the project charter includes a list of those people affected by or who could affect the project. In PM terminology we call these *stakeholders*. Last, the project charter gives authority to the project manager to manage and lead this special endeavor; it passes authority to the PM from the organizational leadership.

Now before we go any further, let me explain something. I have just used several technical terms. I have referred to something called a project charter and I have talked about stakeholders. Regarding the project charter, this is the most frequent name for this document in PM theory. However, if you use other terms within your organization to give a project its initial identity and authority, then use those terms. The question is, have you given a clear identity to the project? Have you identified the main players? If your working environment is more informal, then your project charter may be the declaration written on a piece of paper and tacked to the wall of the office. The project charter is a declaration of the existence of the project. It is important that this declaration be formally documented. Spoken things have a way of fading from view. Written things have more sticking power.

Now our project has an identity and we can proceed. The project charter will eventually lead us into a robust explanation of what specifically we are going to do. We will drill down deep enough to get a thorough understanding of what is needed. But before we go any further defining our mission, let's turn our attentions to some basic tools and structure for our project.

You will need a few tools

We have the project charter that gives our project its identity. Now we need to create some basic tools and give our project a framework to operate in. Think of these as the beginning of a *project infrastructure*. As we look at this structure, you will find some things that are useful and others that are just too much for your situation. I will be addressing only the most essential components needed. Please keep in mind that any formal project environment would include all of the items I am discussing. However, if your situation is markedly informal - a home compared to a small business, for example - you may choose not to use everything discussed. Prune as needed, but before you decide not to use something, try to understand why it is used at all. You may find that you can address the same need in another way more natural to your situation. And that would be just fine.

Talking with each other

How will we talk to each other? How frequently will we interact and have meetings and with whom? When will *status reports* be produced and who will receive them? What venue will be used for reporting, for meetings, and document retention? All of these are important and valid questions. And they are addressed in the *communications plan.* (see appendix) The purpose of the communication plan is to clearly define the expectations of how we will communicate on the project to all parties, all stakeholders. When and how will we talk to each other?

When and how will we communicate? It is important to be perfectly clear when, how, and with whom we will be communicating. Straight-talk and clarity are very important as we build and maintain our relationships with our stakeholders. Given the impact of honesty and transparency as we build team trust, the communications plan is extremely important. This brings clarity around how we plan to talk with each other about things that are fundamental to our project success. The communication plan is a must-have for any project.

> STRAIGHT-TALK AND CLARITY ARE VERY IMPORTANT AS WE BUILD AND MAINTAIN OUR RELATIONSHIPS WITH OUR STAKEHOLDERS

Mapping our progress

How often should we report on the status of the project? Daily? Weekly? Monthly? All of these? What should we report? We will discuss status reporting later in the book, but for now let's simply understand that the status report must include quantitative measures that monitor progress against our project objectives. We should always be able to measure our progress against our goals. For example, how are we doing with the budget, or the remaining tasks? It is essential that there be regular, periodic measurement of how we are doing against our mission's goals. Often times the daily status takes the form of a *15-Minute Daily Stand-up* meeting to rally the team for the day, or could be available as a *Dashboard* for all stakeholders to review. We will address dashboards later, as well. *Weekly Status Checkpoint* meetings typically take the form of the project manager meeting with the team either face-to-face or virtually. The *Monthly Status* meetings are often the venue for executive review or steering committee. However status meetings are structured, they offer a place to regularly review the status of the project. We answer the question: How is the project going?

All eyes on the mission

Status meetings and status reporting are some of the primary tools at your disposal as project manager to keep all eyes on the mission; keep everyone focused on the objective of the project. It is very easy to become distracted by new technologies, possible expanding requirements, team conflicts, or myriad other things. Projects often get mired down in things unrelated to the mission itself. This lack of focus accounts for many project failures. Therefore, it is one

STATUS MEETINGS OFFER A RARE AND INVALUABLE OPPORTUNITY TO THE PROJECT MANAGER TO INSPIRE AND LEAD

of your primary challenges to keep everyone focused on the precise mission before you and to do this purposefully.

Status meetings offer a rare and invaluable opportunity to the project manager to inspire and lead. The various venues and audiences for the different status meetings give the project manager a variety of places from which to encourage and build up the team. Let's explore this.

Open the windows of possibility

Status meetings have a bad rap. Whether we are leading them or are attendees, we typically dread them. They seem for the most part to be bothersome and a waste of time. Oh, we may pick up a bit of information here or there, but on the whole, we think of them as just a necessary fiddle that we have to endure. This should not be the case! They provide the project manager with a regular, and I might say, *spectacular opportunity* to inspire the team as it moves forward.

THEY OFFER THAT RARE CHANCE TO OPEN THE WINDOWS OF POSSIBILITY AND HELP THE TEAM SEE A LITTLE FURTHER INTO THE FUTURE OR REACH A LITTLE HIGHER INTO THE EXCITING WORLD OF AMAZING POSSIBILIES

They offer that rare chance to open the windows of possibility and help the team see a little further into the future or reach a little higher into the exciting world of amazing possibilities.

Whether you are conducting your meetings face-to-face or virtually, you can do this! Let me break it down.

Project status meetings and project status reporting are an ongoing conversation with our stakeholders, an evolving message regarding our journey. Please note that this is an *ongoing conversation* and that it is *evolving*. This means that our status meeting itself is part of a broad fabric of messaging that is developing over time. What about that message?

Our stakeholders – those people having a vested interest in our project – derive a message, intended or not, from the elements of our conversation. So, we have to ask ourselves, what are we saying? We need to be hard on ourselves on this point. What do others *actually* hear from us? Not what precise words did we say, but what was the overall message communicated in words, actions, attitudes? This is what others *hear* from us. We may assume that we are saying one thing, when they are actually hearing something entirely different. What are they hearing from us? Ask them.

> OUR STAKEHOLDERS DERIVE A MESSAGE, INTENDED OR NOT, FROM THE ELEMENTS OF OUR CONVERSATION

Another aspect of this is simply the method of our status reporting. When you look at the sample *Communications Plan* provided in the back of this book, make note of the fact that these examples are for communicating to various types of people. (see appendix) Some stakeholders are highly focused on the raw data and the numbers that drive a situation. They may even want to know the details of calculation and so on. Others are more interested in reading the story. They prefer text, or a narrative account of what is going on. They may even prefer your voice or a face-to-face discussion, rather than text. And still others just want to see a graphic that depicts current project status. The *Weekly Project Status*

Checkpoint and *Monthly Status Reporting* provide project status, giving status with data, text, and graphic. I strongly recommend that project managers speak about status using all of these methods. If we want our message to be heard, we must speak the language that people are hearing.

Our message is formed from three primary sources.

- Intervals of formal communication
- Day-to-day grind
- Elements of the project environment

Depending on the project environment, you have established *intervals of formal communication*. These may include a Daily Standup, Weekly Status Checkpoint, and a Monthly Status Reporting to senior leadership. Weekly and monthly may also involve formal reporting. Each of these carry a message.

As the project continues, you are involved in a *day-to-day grind* of speaking and interacting with others. These are the daily conversations we have with others in the halls, on the phone, or over cubicle walls. And each time we speak, we are carrying a message.

The project itself has a recorded history, a documented life. This is the formal record of the project. These *elements of the project environment* also carry a message. Is the project status message consistent across all sources?

Now the question becomes – what message does the stakeholder hear, and is the message consistent throughout all of our interactions? Is the message clear and transparent? Do our stakeholders know that they can rely on us for a straight answer when the project hits a snag? And do they hear the upbeat rhythm of the numerous little successes your team accomplishes each day? As leaders, the words we say and how we say them conveys a spirit of success or failure, of victory or defeat.

In our status meetings and reporting we look with clarity on the facts of the day. The project information may tell us that we are just fine, or that we are horribly off the track. We take whatever information we have and apply it to our circumstance. At times the message gives us opportunity to cheer. At other times, it calls us to dig deep as a team and work through a difficult season.

BUT NEVER FORGET THAT YOUR TEAM HAS THE POTENTIAL TO AMAZE

But never forget that your team has the potential to amaze. After all, they are *your* team, the best team! The attitude and encouragement you bring as a leader drives the direction of your team. Ultimately, you call them to astonishing results or you call them to some of the same old thing. You must speak the encouraging message you want your people to hear.

An atmosphere of celebration

As the project manager, and more critically, as a *leader*, it is your responsibility to create a vibrant, healthy atmosphere of wonder and discovery. You want to nurture an environment of growth and success. There are many things you can and should do. Here is one idea. Don't wait for an official milestone date or accomplishment to talk about and herald various improvements along the way, quantitative or otherwise. Consider celebrating even the little wins and minor accomplishments, the small, incremental changes and advances of your team. Consider focusing on the forward, positive movement of your people on the project

YOUR VOICE SHOULD ALWAYS BE CREATING AN ENCOURAGING ATMOSPHERE

objectives - the surprising results and innovative solutions they develop, the creativity in a design, or the fitness of a particular application. *Celebrate the good things that are happening!* I am not suggesting that we ignore the real issues and problems. They must all be addressed in a timely and appropriate manner. I am saying, as strongly as I can, that we should be emphasizing the good things that are happening; even as we deal with various challenges we face. Our thought should be that the good message outweighs any other message. We should be speaking about the accomplishments as much or more than the problems that we face. Your voice as the leader should always be creating an encouraging atmosphere where amazing results are regularly achieved and even surpassed. Is this a frivolous waste of your time? Not in the least. In fact, these actions on your part, these encouragements and attention to the attitudes of your team, *directly affect your team's performance*.

What type of team do you have? *You have the best team.* Begin with this view and build on it every day. Remember, *people typically rise to the expectations that we set for them*. If we expect very little, we usually get just that – very little. If we expect much, our people will do their best to meet those

PEOPLE TYPICALLY RISE TO MEET THE EXPECTATIONS THAT WE SET FOR THEM

expectations and even exceed them. They will rise to astonishingly high levels for us – *if we expect them to*. So, do you want the best team? Well, you have it right now. Yes, you have the best. Why? Because they are on *your* project and *you* are their leader. Now be sure and tell them that. Celebrate all the time; the big things and the little things. Let your team know that you care about them and that you appreciate their work.

When the team is healthy, we have successful achievement of milestones on or before their scheduled date, we have improved response times to customer issues and technical support, and we see many performance enhancements as compared to when the team began their work on the project. Plus, your team will know that these advances are deeply appreciated and valued by you and others. They will know this because *you intentionally tell them these things*, you celebrate the wins with them regularly, in a thousand small words and acts as you lead them each day. And these wonderful things that your team is doing will seem to grow cumulatively. Why? Simply because you are constantly *sowing the little seeds of encouragement*, and these seeds begin to bear fruit. As you foster a healthy, enthusiastic environment, it is then that creativity, growth, and invention seem to build right along with it. There is a gathering momentum. But it all begins with your words and attitudes.

Your place to motivate and inspire

Have you ever had an executive or manager who just left you feeling flat? Have you ever been involved in an executive meeting and wondered,

YOUR PRIMARY MISSION IS TO MOTIVATE AND INSPIRE YOUR TEAM

"Jeepers, this is really a waste of my time..." Be assured, you are not alone. But there is more. Did you know that when that happened to you, the executive had *failed* at their primary mission? Really? Yes. You ask, what was their primary mission? Their primary mission - *as a leader* – was to motivate and inspire you. How did they do? Well, they failed, didn't they? The truth is, you *should have* come away from that meeting so charged up, so ready to cram 26 hours into your 24-hour day; you *should have* come away from the meeting pumped and motivated to reach higher and dream bigger; to innovate and create; to produce startling, amazing, wonderful results. But you didn't. You came away flat, wondering how to redeem the lost hour of time.

But here is the important thing. We could probably find an endless spring of examples of poor leadership from the executives we have worked with. They are an easy target for our criticisms. But let's set that all aside. On a project that person is YOU. So, how's it going? How are you doing? On a project, your primary mission is to motivate and inspire your team; to create an atmosphere where anything can happen, where your team does amazing, startling, wonderful things. Do you motivate and inspire? Now, you may say to me, "Yes, but the project has a specific mission..." and so on. But I would say to you, if you truly invest in motivating and inspiring your team, you will achieve your project's objective *and more*, you will achieve your mission *and much more*. Yes, you will achieve much, much more. As a leader, do the first and primary thing. All the rest will follow.

The people we work with

Project results are achieved by groups of people working together. These people working together are called *teams*. When we speak of teams, we are speaking of a certain type of group dynamic highly focused on a defined mission. By contrast, if we have an organization that is structured very top-down, very hierarchical in nature, we do not have a team in the project sense. We have a traditional *working group*. If you spoke with the members of the working group and asked them who was in charge of the group, they would tell you that they *reported to* so-and-so, that they *worked for* so-and-so. By contrast, if you asked a team member the same question, they would likely tell that they *worked with* so-and-so. The team dynamic creates a much stronger sense of equality among the members. The project manager, if anything, is nothing more than the first-among-equals. The project manager has his or her role to play as do each of the team members. This is a subtle but powerful distinction. In addition to our team and the immediate sphere of others working on the project, we have ever-increasing spheres of people getting involved. As we stated earlier, anyone affected by, or who could affect the project, is called a *stakeholder*. So, the universe of stakeholders could potentially be quite large. Yet from a practical perspective we intend to engage only those who are actively engaged in the project effort. Who is involved and who needs to know? It is this more limited universe of stakeholders that we keep informed regarding project status, progress, and so on.

Selecting the team

Teams are selected using a variety of methods. Sometimes the team is comprised of simply those who are available. Sometimes they are preselected and given as a whole - "here's your team" - to the project manager. Sometimes the project manager will carefully select each team member to satisfy the technical requirements of the project. In any case, the team comes together to achieve the stated mission.

Initial challenges

When we think about teams working together, we think about group dynamics. Bruce Tuckman is well-known for his research into this area.[v] He lays out five stages of group development: Forming, Storming, Norming, Performing, and Adjourning/Transforming. Tuckman says that teams move progressively through these phases, and sometimes regress and must make their way through again. During the *Forming stage* there is some ambiguity and uncertainty among the team members. The project manager leads in ways to minimize this and help the team members engage with each other. During the *Storming stage* there arises conflict among the team members. Uncertainties over one's role and individual purpose on the project, confusion over authority, personality clashes, and numerous other conflicts bubble to the surface and challenge the productivity of the group. The Storming stage is a critical juncture for the team members. The project manager must remain engaged and supportive, helping members to relate to each other and helping to resolve conflicts. But the team members themselves must largely work through this period on their own. As they do, it empowers them *as a team* with the skills and abilities to work through the future challenges that they will face. The Storming stage gives them the working knowledge of how to overcome the more difficult future crises that they will encounter. During the *Norming stage* the team members reach a daily rhythm; productive working relationships focused clearly on the project's mission. During the *Performing stage* the team truly seems to coalesce around the project's objective. They become almost super-charged in their razor-sharp focus. All of the solid relationships developed during the Norming stage seem heightened and energized. During the *Adjourning/Transforming stage* the team is acutely aware that the relationships developed up to this point will go through a transition. For some, the changes will seem almost a grieving or mourning. For others, the changes will seem as windows to future opportunities.

Reaching beyond for the summit

We have looked at how teams evolve through Form, Norm, Storm, Perform, and Adjourn. But why do some teams deliver at our minimum expectations while other teams shock us with wonder and amazement? Let's take a few moments and explore this.

Katzenbach and Smith have done a lot of work to understand the things that make for an extraordinary team. In one of their studies they developed the *team performance curve*. In this model they identify four types of teams – Pseudo-team, Potential team, Real team, and Extraordinary team. [vi]

The *pseudo-team* "has not focused on collective

performance and is not really trying to achieve it."[vii] What does this mean in practical terms? It means that the team does not have a clear mission and purpose. They may refer to themselves as *a team*, but yet there is not a defined objective. A team is not a team unless it is focused on the project mission. The pseudo-team is a team in name only. If a team has a team identity without a focus, it is a pseudo-team, and it produces nothing toward the project's objectives.

The *potential team* is "really is trying to improve its performance impact."[viii] This means that the potential team has its eyes on the performance objectives. They have begun to focus on the mission. Let's think about this. If you are leading a pseudo-team (who are delivering nothing) and you begin to call the team to focus on the mission (performance objectives), they become a potential team *simply by beginning to focus* on the mission! This is pretty amazing. All you, as the leader, had to do was help the team focus on the objective. Projects are successful, in part, because the leader keeps the team focused on the project's mission. The potential team produces at a level similar to traditional *working groups*, that is, teams structured in an up-down, hierarchical manner.

The *real team* is "equally committed to a common purpose, goals, and working approach for which they hold themselves mutually accountable."[ix] Now the team life has added a few new dimensions - common purpose, goals, working approach, and mutual accountability. Essentially, the team has added a reasonable structure to support their pursuit of the project's mission. There is a healthy atmosphere on the team as everyone pulls together. The real team outperforms traditional working groups by a large measure. As we move up the team performance curve, the teams have increased impact exponentially. Now, we have one more step – and it is truly out of this world.

The *extraordinary team* has all of the aspects of the real team. They have a project environment that is structured, and they are moving along achieving the project's purpose. But there is something else going on. The extraordinary team has one additional thing in the mix. The team "has members who are also deeply committed to one another's personal growth and success."[x] How do we understand this? It means that each member cares more about their fellow team members than themselves. They care more about the growth and success of their teammates than their own growth and success. They have become less self-centered and more others-centered. Well, that sounds nice, but does it have a performance impact? Yes. In fact, the results coming from an extraordinary team are off-the-charts amazing. Their results are often unexpected and full of invention. The truth is, we cannot predict just how good an extraordinary team will be. We only know that it will be fantastic! So, reach for *extraordinary*.

> EACH MEMBER CARES MORE ABOUT THEIR FELLOW TEAM MEMBERS THAN THEMESELVES. THEY CARE MORE ABOUT THE GROWTH AND SUCCESS OF THEIR TEAMMATES THAN THEIR OWN

As a leader, is it important to grow a project environment that nurtures the team, cares for them, and works to ensure they have the freedom to deliver the very best? Yes, it is. Regardless of where you find your team today, you can lead them up the team performance curve to achieve amazing, startling, wonderful results. It is our charge, our duty, to help our teams be amazing.

Part 2

Get out the shovel and start digging

You need to get specific about your mission. The project charter included a brief description of the project's objective. As we saw, this was a high-level statement addressing your purpose, and not intended to include enough detail to actually do the project. Now we want to get down to the details of the effort involved. At this point we begin to define the specifics of what we are doing. We get down into the details about our mission. Where do we begin?

To begin, let's first talk about what we *do not* want to do. As the project manager you *do not* want to retreat to a solitary location and try to figure this out on your own; you *do not* want to try and define the mission or write out the specifics of what has to be done *on your own*. You may want to write down some ideas; that is fine. But what is most important now, though, is to involve your stakeholders – particularly your team – as many of them as possible. At this point, you need input from the broad spectrum of all those people involved in the project.

Gathering requirements

Gathering requirements engages all of the stakeholders involved in the project. This is potentially a large number of people. Some will be actively engaged in telling what they need (giving requirements), others engaged in interviewing and recording those needs, (getting requirements), and still others engaged in organizing and coordinating this process. Lastly, any stakeholder that is not actively engaged must be passively involved by receiving information on the progress and results of the requirements-gathering effort. All stakeholders must be kept abreast of what is going on, what decisions are being made, how the project requirements are shaping up. There are two primary reasons for having this broad spectrum of stakeholders. First, we want to make sure that the *requirements reflect the wants and needs* of the group we are aspiring to help.

PROJECTS BY THEIR VERY NATURE ARE CHANGE AGENTS

Therefore, we talk to a broad range of those people in an effort to truly understand the requirements. We do not work in isolation. In order to truly understand what others need or want, or how to solve a problem, or what project outcome will address the demands of the marketplace, or whatever the purpose, we need to talk to the real people about the real details. When we say real people, what do we mean? We mean by this that we need to think vertically and go deep into the enterprise, and talk with everyone from the executives to the people who handle the day-to-day, moment-by-moment transactions, the people doing the actual work. We also mean that we must think horizontally and go broadly across the organization to any division, or department, or location that may be affected by our work. Second, we want to *build buy-in among our stakeholders*. What does that mean? It means we want to get a lot of people to *understand* and *agree* that this project is a great idea, that this project meets the needs, solves the problem, or addresses the concerns. It means that we want to build a strong, politically positive view of the project early in the process within the organization impacted by the project. The process begins the moment we walk in the door. This is very important because there is a natural bias to let things run as they have always run. There is a natural bias against any significant change; a bias in favor of the status quo and non-change. Yet projects by their very nature are change agents; they bring change. Consequently, they bring friction. This rubs many people the wrong way. Change makes people uncomfortable. Knowing this, we begin as early as possible to build a positive message around the project. This process involves as many stakeholders as reasonably possible so that we can truly understand the needs and so that we can begin conveying a good message about the changes that are coming.

Marking out the boundaries

Remember, *we are not boiling the ocean*. The propensity of almost every project is to move toward a boiling of the ocean - to try and resolve too big a problem in the limited context of a project. Projects have a defined objective, and within that context, or boundary, our teams will accomplish amazing results. But it is always within the parameters of the project; within our range of scope or mission. How do we mark out the boundaries of our project? We do this by declaring the *assumptions* and *constraints* (see appendix) that we are operating under.

Once the project charter has been agreed to, the team compiles a list of any and all assumptions and constraints concerning the project.

First, let's talk about *assumptions*. What are these, you ask? Assumptions are statements declaring what is or is not within the project scope. If there is any area of potential confusion as to whether it is *in scope* or *out of scope*, then it should be declared as in or out in the assumptions. Our assumptions list addresses any area of potential confusion by declaring specifically that something is either in or out of scope. The assumptions list can be quite lengthy in a complex environment. It need not be exhaustive but must address potential areas of confusion relative to the project. Most assumptions are acknowledged early in the project definition. However, it is possible to add to the list along the way if areas of confusion present themselves.

Second, let's talk about *constraints*. Projects exist within a larger organization. The enterprise has specific aspects that will impact the project. For example, the technical infrastructure is of a certain design that may or may not accommodate the activities of the project. The enterprise calendar may have periods of time when the system is not available, when the system is frozen from technical updates during peak or sensitive periods of time. Or the objective of the project is to deliver the result prior to an organizational event like a product release or a marketing tradeshow. Constraints are any special aspects that need to be noted, accounted for, and mapped in the project team's thinking. As with the assumptions list, the constraint list need not be exhaustive, but must address any potential areas of conflict relative to the project.

Most constraints are acknowledged early in the project definition, as well. However, it is possible to add to the list along the way if new constraints are discovered.

Open discussion and awareness of assumptions and constraints are important to the health of the project. Stakeholders help us establish them. Successful focus on the project objective is accomplished, in part, by clarity on what is in scope or out of scope, and by a clear declaration of any assumptions or constraints to the project. The assumptions and constraints mark our boundaries around the project objective. Our mission gains considerable clarity when this has been done. And as the project proceeds, when areas of confusion or fuzziness begin to erode the team's focus on mission, consider adding an assumption or constraint to more tightly bound the objective. Assumptions and constraints are often required to provide needed clarity to the project's objective.

The best project in the world

How do you feel about this project? As the project manager are you excited? If not, then it is unlikely that your team will be. To be sure, not every project has the same wow-factor and excitement. But as the project manager and leader you set the tone for the team. Your attitudes shape the attitudes of the team as whole. With this in mind, you must radiate a hopefulness and excitement about what you are doing. You must be regularly proclaiming the reasons why this project is the best project in the world.

Exactly how big is it?

Make a detailed list of everything

As specific requirements are gathered from the stakeholders, a detailed list is created. This is the *requirements list*. Often a spreadsheet is created and used for this purpose. (see appendix) Each of the listed requirements includes a description of the requirement, an owner who we can go to for more detail, and a decision whether the requirement is included in or excluded from the project objectives. If excluded, some stakeholders further break things down to various categories for future considerations. This list of requirements is a principal document as we develop a detailed understanding of what we are doing on this project.

Now you have a substantial list of all of the wants and needs and desires of a good number of stakeholders. Some of these things will become part of the final project and some will not. The important thing at this point is that you have been listening to everyone. You have not been making prejudgments about what should or should not be a part of the project. By the way, when we truly listen and do not come with preconceptions of outcome, *this is where our stakeholders begin to trust us*. This is where our stakeholders begin to see that our efforts are on their behalf, not our own - *on their behalf.* They begin to see that we are doing this project to meet their needs, not our own - *their needs.* Therefore, we need to come to these conversations absolutely transparent and open to a variety of outcomes.

Remember, when everyone is doing the initial gathering, they are doing just that – *gathering* – not selecting – they are *gathering*. They are listening and taking note of what others believe is needed. They are not making decisions about the shape and magnitude of the project – just listening and taking notes. It is during this gathering of requirements that many new and innovative ideas come out. When you have so many people contributing to the mix of ideas, often some truly wonderful things are discovered. This is just another big incentive to listen and not interpret.

Now, this substantial list of initial requirements is reviewed by the stakeholders. Often a representative group of stakeholders is selected to speak on behalf of the broad constituency of all the stakeholders. Nevertheless, the stakeholders together review the initial list of requirements. They go through them one by one. They discuss and debate the merits or not of each one. Some are identified as right in line with the aim and purpose of the project, and others are found to be lacking. Those that map to the objectives of the project, that help us accomplish the mission, become *approved requirements*. That is to say, the stakeholders begin to define specifically what we will do. The other things listed on our initial requirements gathering are not viewed as being within our scope. They do not align with the objectives of the project. These are set aside as *exclusions*. By the way, many exclusions are indeed very notable suggestions, and you would want to retain the ideas for future use. Also, this is not a place for brokering compromises between requirements. Namely, conversations like – "I give you this" and "you give me that". Remember, we have a broadly defined mission in our project charter. The only question before us is: what are the details that comprise that broader objective; what specifics help us achieve our mission? So as to our specific mission on this project, after looking at each requirement and making a determination of whether it is part of the project objectives or not, the stakeholders agree that this final list establishes the approved requirements of the project. These *approved requirements* are the *scope* of the project. This is an important step. Establishing the scope of the project, the breadth and detail of what we are being asked to do, is a critical step in all successful projects. You must have a scope in order to move forward. An understanding of scope is required whether you are going to move forward in a traditional waterfall approach or lean agile.

Let's be very clear. At this point all stakeholders have agreed what the approved requirements are. All stakeholders have agreed what we are being asked to do, and what we are agreeing to accomplish in the project. All stakeholders have agreed on the project scope. Now, lock this definition down. Lock it down! We formally call this the project's *scope baseline*. It is nothing less than the very definition of *what it means to be "done"; what it means to finish the project*. This is very important. The scope baseline is

THE VERY DEFINITION OF WHAT IT MEANS TO BE DONE; WHAT IT MEANS TO FINISH THE PROJECT

the definitive statement of specifically what we are doing to meet the project objectives. Once the requirements have been agreed to and once scope has been accepted by all stakeholders, no additions or alterations of any kind are made to what we are doing unless it goes through formal *change management*. Once the project scope baseline has been established and accepted, no changes are made to the definition of what we are doing unless it goes through the change management process (more about this later). Why? Because *scope creep*, or out-of-control project scope, is where many, if not most, projects fail. Project scope creep is one of your primary enemies. Managing project scope is one of the most basic and effective things any project manager can do to assure that his or her project will be successful. Start here.

Now that we have our project details and our project scope baseline is locked down, we are ready to move forward. Let's grab that approved list of requirements, the project's scope baseline, and take things to another level.

I am not sure how this will turn out.

Now I am going to throw a wrench into the works. We just talked about making a detailed list of everything. But some of you are not sure exactly how your project will proceed or even how it will end. It may be that your business is evolving, or the marketplace is changing around you, or – for whatever reason – you just don't have all the details yet. This brings us to a discussion of our overall approach.

There are two main project management approaches.

One is the *waterfall approach* and the other is the *agile* or *lean approach*. Waterfall has been with us the longest, agile is a more recent development. Many companies employ a hybrid of the two – their own style - a little waterfall here and a dash of agile there - something that works for them. Frankly, hybrid approaches are the most common today. There are reasons to emphasize one over the other, though, so take note and have the best of both worlds available to employ.

Let me paint a broad picture of each approach. Along the way, I will describe what circumstances merit using one or the other – or both if you want to be creative!   There is no single approach that is right in every situation. What is important here is for us to understand them and the situations where they are most helpful.

To get started, we must have a clear notion of the *project life cycle*. PMI®[xi] describes a generic project life cycle as comprised of four basic sequential phases:

- Starting the project
- Organizing and preparing
- Carrying out the project work
- Closing the project

OK, that was pretty simple. Now let's peel it back a bit.

Project life cycle mirrors closely the *project management process*. PMI®[xii] defines this process as:

- Initiating
- Planning
- Executing

- Monitoring and Controlling
- Closing

Now this is beginning to sound familiar. These five processes are those typically employed within business today in one form or another as a general project management structure. They sketch a broad outline from launch to completion. Whether waterfall or agile, projects evolve through these processes over time. Here's a suggestion. As you organize your project (more on this later), these five processes provide a ready-made structure. Use it.

In everyday speak, project life cycle and project management process are thought of as more or less synonymous terms. Now let's examine both waterfall and agile and the somewhere in-between..

The *waterfall approach* is characterized by cascading, like a waterfall, from start to finish, through the *project life cycle* phases and through the tasks. The project moves sequentially and systematically from beginning to the end. It moves through initiating, planning, executing, monitoring and controlling, and closing. It is structured in a detailed level on tasks and activities.

When should we use waterfall? Here are the circumstances when the waterfall approach is the appropriate choice.

- When you have a clear understanding of where you want to go, when the finished end state is clearly understood, and when the triple constraints of scope, cost, and schedule are known

- When you know exactly what you want, and all of the requirements are clearly understood or are available to the team during development

- Typically associated with a long-term investment in an envisioned permanent solution

- The solution is available at project conclusion when its productivity will be realized

The *agile approach* is characterized by its iterative nature, moving through oftentimes daily iterations of development. Imagine cycling, repeatedly moving through planning, executing, monitoring and controlling. Over and over and over in small bites. With each iteration the team achieves a *good enough* version of executable work that is immediately promoted into production. Although agile follows through the *project life cycle* phases, it iterates countless times within the life cycle, intentionally cycling in a loop, until the sponsor is satisfied. It is structured on a detailed level based on stories or scenarios.

When should we use agile? Here are the circumstances when the agile approach is the appropriate choice.

- When you do not have a clear understanding of where you want to go, and things are evolving and changing as the project proceeds

- When you do not know exactly what you want, and the requirements are understood progressively, day-by-day, as the team evolves the solution

- Typically associated with a short-term investment that may involve on going reinvestment in cost and schedule

- The solution evolves throughout the project and is productively realized along the way

Now that we have had a brief glimpse at waterfall and agile approaches, what about a hybrid of both, a little of mixing them together? To be honest, hybrid is what is most commonly used in today's environment. Although many companies *say* they are an agile shop, they are actually operating as a hybrid environment. Let me give just a few examples. Some companies find great benefit in carefully defining their requirements at the beginning of a project (unlike an agile approach that discovers it along the way), but also have found that a few agile techniques are useful such as a brief daily stand-up meeting, or *scrum.* This is a hybrid. Other companies develop the form and shape of the solution along the way (gradually unpacking the requirements in an agile way). Yet, they do not promote to production with every cycle – and may be waiting until the end of the project (which is undefined in an agile effort until you get there). This is a hybrid. The point in this is that we should pull from waterfall or agile as we have need. The team should help us structure the project early on, and we can adjust things as our project moves forward.

In recent years PMI® has given additional clarity around project life cycle. They have further refined the traditional waterfall-agile-hybrid conversation into five distinct development life cycles. The beauty is that we are not locked into a few options but are at liberty to choose an approach that most effectively accomplishes our given mission. Here is what PMI® says.

Project life cycles can be predictive or adaptive. Within a project life cycle, there are generally one or more phases that are associated with the development of the product, service, or result. These are called a development life cycle. Development life cycles can be predictive, iterative, incremental, adaptive, or a hybrid model:

- In a predictive life cycle, the project scope, time, and cost are determined in the early phases of the life cycle. Any changes to the scope are carefully managed. Predictive life cycles may also be referred to as waterfall life cycles.

- In an iterative life cycle, the project scope is generally determined early in the project life cycle, but time and cost estimates are routinely modified as the project team's understanding of the product increases. Iterations develop the product through a series of repeated cycles, while increments successively add to the functionality of the product.

- In an incremental life cycle, the deliverable is produced through a series of iterations that successively add functionality within a predetermined time frame. The deliverable contains the necessary and sufficient capability to be considered complete only after the final iteration.

- Adaptive life cycles are agile, iterative, or incremental. The detailed scope is defined and approved before the start of an iteration. Adaptive life cycles are also referred to as agile or change-driven life cycles.

- A hybrid life cycle is a combination of a predictive and an adaptive life cycle. Those elements of the project that are well known or have fixed requirements follow a predictive development life cycle, and those elements that are still evolving follow an adaptive development life cycle.

It is up to the project management team to determine the best life cycle for each project.[xiii]

There we have an overview of the various approaches in project life cycle. Much more could be said, but I will leave that to your individual research and applications. Here, in our study, we are drawing the broad outlines. Again, there is no single approach that is right in every situation. It is important for us to understand each of them and the situations where they can be best utilized. Then you are free to blend them as you have need.

Make the big thing small

Now we go back to our *detailed list of everything*. We have our arms full of detailed, approved requirements. Our requirements list may be a modest list of fifteen requirements needed to satisfy our planning for very simple effort, or it may involve a list of thousands of requirements needed to develop a new software application. Now what do we do? How do we begin to organize this huge pile? Quite simple. We break things down into workable pieces, workable sizes. What does this mean? Let me explain with an example.

My sons can teach us all about it

When my children were young, I was occasionally recruited to help them clean their rooms. I remember how things typically went – especially with each of my sons. We would go to the bedroom - the project site location - and survey the disaster. Breathtaking. If you are a parent of young children, then you know. It is almost unimaginable how much in disarray a room can become under the supervision of small boys. But... we pressed on. I glanced quickly around and said, "OK, throw all the stuffed animals in a pile on the bed." Then I said, "And the books, pick up and put on the book shelves... Oh, and the tapes and CDs can go on the media rack." Then I caught my breath and said, "Yeah, and throw the dirty clothes out into the hallway into a pile." I spun around and gasped, "... and the trash put in the trash basket." Then I caught my balance and began to relax a little. I might add here that anytime you give your kids permission to throw things – this is a win in their eyes - the stuffed animals, the clothes, the trash! All good. By now, the only things remaining were some miscellaneous bits and pieces which I would not know how to organize. And it is at this point in the process that they would look up and say something like, "Dad, I really don't need you here. I can do this myself." Cool. I was hoping for that. Each son, in his time, was taking control of his situation.

But let's think about the process. My sons and I were confronted with disorder and confusion. All I did was provide some broad categories to help them organize their things. I provided some groups, some categories of things to help bring order to an otherwise disorganized situation. Together my sons and I broke the work down into workable pieces. But believe me, on projects, it is no different. It is the same process. When things start to look too confusing, just remember – you are organizing a messy room – nothing more.

The same thing

Whether you have fifteen requirements in your project or thirty-five hundred requirements, it is the same. We break everything down. It is all a question of magnitude. If the situation seems just out of this world, then take a deep breath and slowly move forward. We take the big unwieldy thing, the massive list of approved requirements, and we break these down into smaller, more manageable pieces. But into what categories or groups? That is entirely up to you and your team. Whatever makes sense to you. Whatever seems logical or helps the team keep things straight. Don't concern yourself with the order in which the pieces need to be done. Just break the work down into pieces the team can handle. We call this the *work breakdown structure*. A simple example may help us here.

Let's imagine that your project is to paint a room in your house. As you think about all of the details surrounding this fairly simple, everyday project, your eyes begin to glaze over. Let's see: select the paint for walls, select the paint for window trim, buy the paint, prepare the wall surfaces, buy other materials needed, apply masking tape along the floor and window molding, test the ceiling paint, test the trim paint, test the wall paint, paint the ceiling, paint the trim, paint the walls, wait for paint to dry, test paint dryness, touch up as needed, remove the masking tape, and clean up the mess. And we could go on. We could get into much more detail on even this relatively simple project. But for now, let's just consider what we have. We could take all of these details (and any amount of detail beneath this) and we could summarize it into four categories: 1) Buy paint and supplies, 2) Prepare the site and surfaces, 3) Paint the room, and 4) Clean up the site.

AS PROJECT MANAGERS AND LEADERS, WE MUST UNDERTAKE THESE THINGS WITH THE HELP OF OUR TEAM

Each of these groups describes one or more actions that will be taken as part of the project. They are all actions – *doing* kinds of things. For example, *Prepare the site and surfaces* includes making sure the site is free of obstacles, that all other surfaces are reasonably protected with drop cloths, that floor and window moldings are protected with masking tape, and that the wall surfaces have been cleaned and prepared for new paint. So, in the case of my room painting project, although I can drill down into greater and greater levels of detail, I have four initial categories or groups of actions. I have four groups of actions or verbs. I have four work packages. *Work packages* are nothing more complex than summarized groups of tasks; groups of the actions I will be taking. Look at the work packages for the painting project: Buy,

Prepare, Paint, Clean up. Four sets of actions. Work packages are typically organized as *phases*, and within phases there are *activities*, and within activities there are *tasks*, and within tasks there are *subtasks*, and sub-subtasks, and so on. After we have broken things down into our initial categories, or work packages, then we decompose each work package down to the lowest possible level where no task is bigger than then can be managed effectively. Avoid work packages that are too large to manage. Things like project management activity and ongoing support are represented as blocks of time that are parsed out over the duration of the effort. They may be quite large, but they represent a metered release of effort over the project life. This structure of work packages - beginning with the high-level and decomposing down to the lowest possible level of task - is called the *work breakdown structure* or *WBS*.

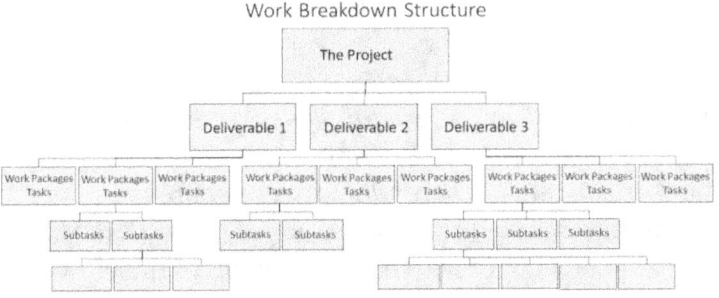

Work Breakdown Structure

Let's pause right here to make a point of emphasis once again. As project managers and leaders, we must undertake these things with the help of our team. As we break things down into workable pieces, into broad meaningful categories, we must do this with our team's advice. As we decompose each work package into greater and greater levels of detail, smaller and smaller tasks, we must do this with our team's insight and advice. As project managers and leaders, we should always be engaging the thoughts and ideas of our team. We need their help. As we actively engage the imagination of our people in everything we are doing, we not only gain their support and strong endorsement, but we remain open to the creativity of each person. Again, as a leader, we must always be sowing seeds of inspiration and motivation.

AS A LEADER, WE MUST ALWAYS BE SOWING SEEDS OF INSPIRATION AND MOTIVATION

The work breakdown structure covers everything

So, your work package has been decomposed down to a level where no task is bigger than 40-80 hours. Now what? We need to press in on one particular point. Does this *work breakdown structure* (WBS) cover everything? Ask the question, because it must. The WBS must be another *equivalent expression* of your approved requirements, or your scope baseline. The WBS covers the same breadth of activity and content as the project scope. These must all be equal. Why?

Very soon the WBS will be used to establish our *cost baseline* and our *schedule baseline*. If the WBS is not equivalent to the *scope baseline*, then there will be inconsistencies between our three baselines. They will not map to each other. They will not reflect each other. Therefore, we press the point that the WBS must represent the content of the scope baseline - *completely*.

Let me mention one important area that is often overlooked: administrative activities. Specifically, project management activities are frequently overlooked. These must be reflected in your WBS. Why? Again, the WBS is the basis for building our cost and schedule baselines. If we fail to include something in the WBS, *there will not be time and there will not be money* to do it. So, I leave you with a question. As

> AS WE ACTIVELY ENGAGE THE IMAGINATION OF OUR PEOPLE IN EVERYTHING WE ARE DOING, WE NOT ONLY GAIN THEIR SUPPORT AND STRONG ENDORSEMENT, BUT WE REMAIN OPEN TO THE CREATIVITY OF EACH PERSON

the project manager, do you like being paid for your work? Of course, you do. But if you fail to include your project management activities in the WBS, then you will have no funds to pay yourself. Sorry for you. So, plan to pay yourself. Include administration and support in the WBS. You understand my point. The WBS needs to have everything in it that you will be doing on the project. By the way, did you include a celebration party to commemorate the project success at the end? You should. It is always surprising to us how these little things heighten our team's performance. The scheduled celebration may be just that little extra something that drives your team forward to press in hard at the end of the project with the greatest momentum. Is there a cost?

Of course, there is. Is it worth it? Immeasurably. The performance gains from simply showing your team that you care about them are very substantial indeed. Plan for it now and you will have the time and money at the end. Show your team that you have them in mind from the very beginning and all along the way.

Part 3

The cost of everything

With our work breakdown structure (WBS) in hand, we are ready to tackle several other things. Before we do, though, let's consider one critical aspect of project management thought.

The triple constraints

By this point in our discussions, we have at least mentioned the three baselines. In project management thinking we talk about the *triple constraints*, or the project management triangle. This means that we are talking about the three baselines that are used to manage a project: scope baseline, cost baseline, and schedule baseline. So far in our discussions here, we have addressed only the scope baseline. All of these baselines are interlocked. That is, they are *constrained* by each the other. For example, I cannot change my scope without affecting my cost and schedule. I cannot change any of the baselines without affecting the others. In fact, one can easily see there are *infinite possibilities of variation* in all of this. And this leads to the complexity that is the challenge in the project management environment. At this point it is clear that we also need to understand both the cost baseline and the schedule baseline in order to effectively manage and lead projects.

Project Triple Constraints

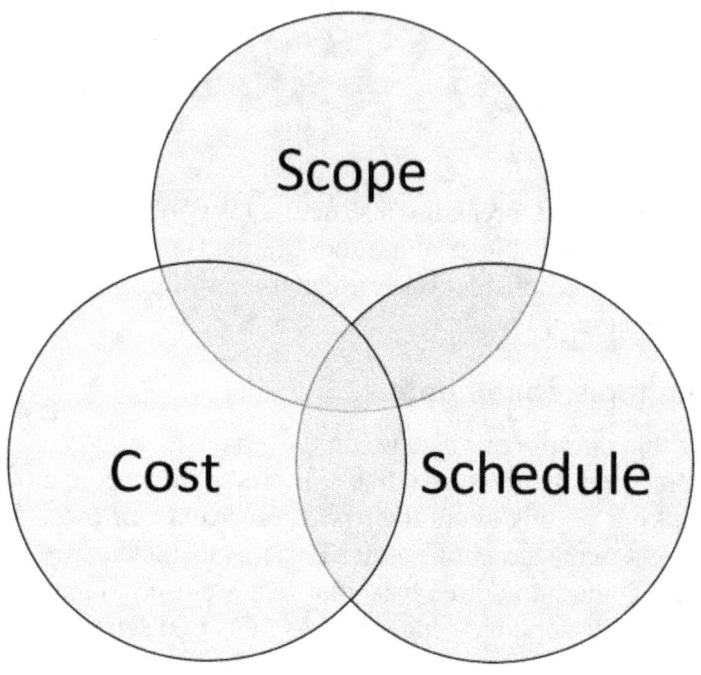

They are mutually dependent
A change in one constraint impacts the others

The cost of the project

In many working environments projects are assigned an initial budget. These may be in the form of legal contracts, internal agreements, or simply an initial working estimate. What is important is that this initial budget should be held loosely until the cost baseline is formally established and accepted by the stakeholders. It is frequently the case that initial project estimates are pretty rough. Remember that during the requirements analysis, the stakeholders were carefully listening and taking note of needs. Consequently, as the requirements analysis seeks to define the details of the project scope, and as those requirements are more fully understood, initial notions on cost are often found to have been not very accurate. As we work through how we find the cost baseline, it should become clear how this happens. So, let's take a look at how we establish the cost baseline.

Costs are rooted in the work breakdown structure

Once we had identified our list of approved requirements, we reorganized these into workable pieces. That is to say, we grouped, or reordered, them in ways meaningful to us so that we could manage them more effectively. That done, we also expanded the details of each of those things into tasks that were no bigger than 40-80 hours. And this gave us an understanding and a view of a level of the task sufficiently detailed enough to properly manage the work. Now what? We begin our cost analysis at the lowest level of tasks available in the WBS.

Is it effort or duration?

Let's imagine that my phone rings and I answer it. "Hello," I say.

The voice on the other end of the line tells me that he has 40 hours of programming work. And he asks if I can come on Monday morning and start work.

I say, "Hey, I love a challenge. I'll see you then!" And I hang up the phone.

So, on Monday morning I show up, and my caller walks up to me with an armful of papers. "Here are your programming specifications. I'll see you on Friday afternoon." And he turns to walk away.

I call after him, "Hey, wait a minute. I'll see you two weeks from now on Friday afternoon." And I turn to walk away.

Then he calls after me, "Wait a minute. You don't understand. That is 40 hours of programming work. I will see you this Friday afternoon."

Then I said, "Please excuse me, but you don't understand. I am only here 50% of the time. I have something else going on in the afternoon. So, I will see you two weeks from now."

"Oh," he says, "I see! You are only available 50% of the time. I will see you in two weeks."

What was happening? We were miscommunicating over the concepts of *effort* and *duration*. My caller had offered me forty hours of programming *effort*, or work. I said it would take me ten days to complete it, meaning ten days of *duration*. In my ten days I was taking into account eight hours per day and a five-day week. Plus, I was factoring in my availability of only 50%.

When we speak about cost and the *cost baseline*, we are speaking about the *effort*. How much actual work will it take to complete a given task? Generally, this is expressed in hours. Effort considers the task alone without regard to the calendar. Simply put, how long will this task take to complete? By contrast, when we speak about scheduling and the *schedule baseline*, we are speaking about *duration*. How long will this task take *in calendar time*? How long will this task take looking at a calendar? In simple terms, duration is the combined consideration of effort and availability. One might also bring productivity into consideration. So, we have effort and duration. Effort we will use as we calculate our cost baseline. Duration we will use as we calculate our schedule baseline.

Start at the bottom and roll it up

Using our WBS, we go to the lowest level task, a level providing enough detail, and we estimate how long the task will take to complete. Let's stop right here and reemphasize a key point. As the project manager, we must never assume that we can develop these estimates in isolation from our team. Our team members are our group of experts. We must rely on them

NEVER ASSUME THAT WE CAN DEVELOP THESE ESTIMATES IN ISOLATION FROM OUR TEAM

for these estimates. And, yes, we should convey to them our confidence that they will provide good numbers to us. That said, let's continue. As we work through each task and each estimate, the estimates are aggregated upward, level by level, into a project total. From the bottom of the WBS to the top. We called this a *bottom-up estimate*. Bottom-up estimates are the most accurate of all estimates given because they take into consideration each task individually. By comparison, the *top-down estimate* is often available, but less precise.

These estimates may be initial estimates made by sales teams, engineering, or others looking to establish a preliminary idea of costs. But they are not as accurate as the bottom-up estimates which takes into account the detailed efforts involved.

This bottom-up estimate represents our cost baseline. This means that the cost baseline is a reflection of the cost to accomplish the scope baseline. They are *equal* but unique perspectives of our project. Stated differently, our *scope* can be accomplished for the *cost* within the *schedule* we have all agreed on.

THIS IS A HEALTHY STEP IN THE NORMAL PROCESS OF BRINGING OUR BASELINES INTO AGREEMENT

Now, an interesting thing often happens at this point. Frequently the cost baseline is quite different from, and often much larger than, any initial estimates or even formal contracts that have been agreed to. What does this tell us? It informs us that our scope baseline, the list of approved requirements, is out of sync with our understanding of cost. It tells us that we must reconcile this disparity before proceeding. By the way, this is not a bad thing, at all. This is *a healthy step in the normal process of bringing our baselines into agreement*. Fine, you say. Now what? What do we do when this occurs? It is simple. Either initial estimates or contract amount must be changed to substantially agree with the new findings, or the scope baseline must be reduced to agree with these conclusions. Either we agree to spend more, or we agree to do less. Keep in mind that we also need to reconcile the schedule baseline against any initial schedule expectations that exist and bring the schedule baseline into agreement with our scope.

Now that our scope and cost baselines is in agreement, we are in a position to proceed. We turn our attentions to the schedule.

Laying it out on a calendar

We again take our work breakdown structure, our WBS, and use it to help us build our project schedule. And again, we go to the lowest task in the structure and evaluate each of the lowest tasks. As you remember, we are thinking of the *duration* of each task - the combined consideration of effort and availability. How long will the task take given the availability of the resources on a calendar? And if you have productivity in your calculations, that is fine, too. Once we have the duration for each of our lowest tasks in the structure, we are ready to proceed.

What comes before what, what comes after what

In order to establish our schedule, we need to understand precedence. What comes before what, and what comes after what? More specifically, we need to understand *precedence diagramming method* (PDM). What are the relationships between the tasks that allow one thing to happen before another, or permits things to move in parallel, or requires that several tasks begin at the same time, and so on. All of these types of questions, and many more, are addressed in our understanding of PDM and precedence relationships.

To get started on our schedule, let's return to the WBS. When we developed the work breakdown structure, we purposely did not consider the sequence of events. In fact, our purpose at that time was simply to organize groups of things into more workable, more manageable pieces. If we consider our illustrated WBS from earlier, we see that our project has been structured under our *deliverables*, those products or services produced by the project. We noted earlier that these were things *(nouns)* that were produced by the project. Next, each deliverable has a number of actions *(verbs)* beneath it. These actions are the tasks required to complete the deliverable. Now we take all of the actions, all the verbs, all of the tasks, and reorder them with the sequence of events in mind. What must be done first and second and third and so on. This analysis involves only tasks, or verbs, only *doing kinds of things,* or actions. It does not involve deliverables, or nouns. We are only concerned with *when* we can do things. We reorder all of the tasks, from beginning to end, in the order that they must be completed. There is often a lot of freedom here. The project manager should feel *compelled to involve every member* of the team in these deliberations.

YOU NEED THE THOUGHTS AND INSIGHTS OF YOUR TEAM ALL THE WAY THROUGH - YOUR TEAM UNDERSTANDS MANY MORE OF THE SUBTLE NUANCES BETWEEN VARIOUS TASKS THAN YOU WILL EVER KNOW

Let's pause again to stress a key point that we have emphasized multiple times before. You, as the project manager, are *not working in isolation* on the schedule. You need the thoughts and insights of your team all of the way through. Your team understands many more of the subtle nuances between various tasks than you will ever know. It is critical to the project's success that you engage them actively in this process. Do not come to them with a schedule in hand and ask them to simply approve what you have figured out for them. Rather, involve them in the task-by-task process of building the schedule, the detailed decisions; ask for their input. Your actions will illustrate to each of the team members the value you put on their thoughts. It will show them how much you *trust* them. And it will ultimately earn their *buy-in* on the project schedule that you are committing them to.

Now the team tells you, "Wait a minute! I cannot start this task until another one is complete." Or they say, "I could work on these tasks in parallel, and that could save time." Or they say, "I must have this single resource to do these critical tasks, and yet this person is needed on many other tasks throughout the project. It seems like that may slow down our schedule." This is exactly the kind of feedback you need among your team right now. Does this complicate the process? Yes, enormously. Is it necessary? Absolutely! Without this type of critique, interplay, and challenge; without this type of hard, aggressive inquiry, the project schedule will not be properly confirmed and verified. It will not reflect reality. Without your team's help, you will never adequately establish a solid project *schedule baseline*.

We mentioned earlier that once we calculate the cost baseline derived from our WBS, we often find a disconnect between the original cost expectations and the results of summing up all of the combined effort in the planned tasks. And we pointed out that this was not uncommon, but that these figures needed to be reconciled. Likewise, with the schedule baseline.

There is often some initial expectation of when the project will be completed, or perhaps even an anticipated milestone schedule. And, as in the case of cost expectations, our schedule expectations may also be a part of a legal contract, other internal understandings, or even tied to an event such as a convention or market release or seasonal calendar. Whatever the source of the expectation, your analysis of this project may find a disconnect between initial expectations and the realities in the project itself. As with our cost considerations, this informs us that our scope baseline, the list of approved requirements, is out of sync with our understanding of the schedule. It tells us that we must reconcile this disparity before proceeding. And again, this is not a bad thing, at all. This is a *part of the normal process of bringing our baselines into agreement*. And what do we do when this occurs? The same as before. Either initial time estimates or contract schedules must be changed to substantially agree with the new findings or the scope baseline expectations must be changed to agree with these conclusions. Either we agree to take more time or we agree to do less. There are no other choices on the table.

Some people want to live in unreality

Some of you may be quietly smiling to yourself, wondering where I have been living all of my life. Because, you say, some people will not accept a change, *any change*, to the initial expectations. They will not consider a change in cost or schedule. They will not consider a change to the contract or agreement or an understanding of how we will get to the end point. Some people will not accept this, you say. And I agree. There are some people who will not accept any shift in the original expectations regardless of whether it is based on a detailed analysis of what we are doing or not. They simply will not accept a change. So, how do we handle this? This is yet another project management situation that further complicates the environment. But we must address it.

Let us begin by *not presuming* that change is unacceptable. It may be that our detractor does not understand the breadth or details of the situation. I suggest the following approach. Go to your detractor and thank them for the opportunity to lead this project. Then talk in general terms about how you – *as a team* – always confirm the stakeholder's requirements in the early stages of a project. You gather facts. Point out that this detailed analysis has discovered that the scope envisioned by the stakeholders was not supported by either the cost, or schedule, or both. And give them the basic information grounded in your analysis. Let them know that you are excited to proceed, but that your team will need clarity around the *proposed* baselines. Specifically, you will need less scope or more cost and/or more schedule. The best of all situations is that your detractor will see the logic of what you are saying and accept it. They will either reduce the requirements or give you more time and/or money. This is, of course, the ideal scenario.

But we all know that things don't always go that way. What if they reject the team's analysis and will not budge? What if they will not accept reality? What if, in the face of facts and details to the contrary, they will not accept any change to the project whatsoever? Then you must accept this difficult circumstance and move forward. The critical thing in this circumstance is to speak honestly, relating the facts, and give a clear course of proposed action.

SPEAKING TRUTHFULLY, ESPECIALLY IN CRISIS MOMENTS, BUILDS THE TEAM'S TRUST IN YOU AND DEMONSTRATES TO THE SPONSOR THAT YOU CAN TRULY BE TRUSTED

Speaking truthfully, especially in crisis moments, builds the team's trust in you and demonstrates to the sponsor that you can truly be trusted even when the news is bad. If your detractor will not accept the reality of the situation, then you must enter an additional *risk* into your project. Your detractor will not appreciate this, but you have a responsibility to speak and report honestly about conditions on the project. Of course, these risks will periodically be reviewed by our stakeholders and sponsors including senior leadership. Now, we have not spoken of *risk management* yet. But we will shortly. Suffice it to say that we must enter a *risk* into our *risk log*. And then we track this risk regularly. In this way, the inherent disconnect in our baselines will become an ongoing conversation and focal point among stakeholders and sponsors. This is what you do as a project manager. You are tracking any exposure – risks included - to project success. You are watching for indications of failure. Remember, there are basic principles at work in the project management environment including the triple constraints, our three baselines. These baselines must agree with each other. Scope, cost, and schedule baselines must be in sync. So, in order to track the project accurately and optimize the project's chances of success, the triple constraints must be in agreement.

WITHOUT LEADERSHIP CONTROL OF THE BASELINES, YOUR SCOPE, COST, AND SCHEDULE WILL GROW UNABATED

Without leadership control of the baselines, your scope, cost, and schedule will grow unabated. Things can quickly move out of control and off the tracks. *Baseline control is at the center of solid project management.* Therefore, this risk, although an irritant to your detractor, is critically important to monitor regularly. It is always possible that your detractor may, in time, see the wisdom of approving a change in plans in order to reduce the risk of project failure.

Plans, milestones, and, charts

Sometimes a client will come to me and say, "When can I see the breakdown structure?" I am always intrigued by this question, so I respond, "Tell me what you mean by 'breakdown structure.' I want to be sure I provide you with what you have in mind." Then they proceed to describe a typical project plan without the dates, estimated hours, or resource detail. They are simply interested in the tasks I have in mind for the project. In other words, they want to see a preliminary project plan; they are looking for a sense of the basic approach that will be used to handle their situation. But what else do we see in this? Namely, that the WBS is basically transferable, as a structure, over to our project plan. Of course, we need to think through any *dependencies* that exist between various tasks, various work packages. But essentially when you apply precedence considerations to a WBS, you get the project plan.

Building the network view

Now let's think about the order in which we will do the tasks in our project. In order to properly sequence our tasks, we use a specific technique. We call this the *precedence diagramming method (PDM)*[xiv]. This is sometimes referred to as a network diagram. Remember, we are only working with the tasks, actions, or the doing kinds of things. There are four precedence relationships used in project management theory. The most common relationship is Finish-to-Start (FS). That is to say, we finish one thing, and we start another. Another relationship is Finish-to-Finish (FF). Which is to say, we finish two or more tasks at the same time. Another is the relationship Start-to-Start (SS). Lastly, is the relationship Start-to-Finish (SF). That is, you start a thing, and we finish another. This is not commonly used, but it does exist. With these things in mind, let me mention another important principle as you work through these considerations. I recommend that you have *as few special situations as possible*. First, remember that the basic precedence relationship is FS. This is the default of all project management software. I recommend that you keep your tasks naturally ordered (from top to bottom, first to last – in precedence order) as you build the project plan. I recommend that you have as few abnormal dependencies (unusual branching from one place to another) and as few unusual precedence relationships of SS and FF as possible. This will minimize your ongoing maintenance on the project plan. Many project plans get very convoluted over the life of the project. *Strive to keep your plans as simple as possible.* You will thank yourself every day. Naturally, you can't entirely avoid unusual situations. They happen. But I am suggesting that you begin with as simple of a project plan as you can. Over time, undoubtedly, you will introduce things here and there. But start simple. And strive to keep it as simple as possible.

I emphasize, once again, that these considerations, this precedence diagram, should be developed with the team's active engagement. They are the experts. The precedence diagram drives your schedule. A realistic schedule is grounded in the insights of your team.

Once created, the project plan offers the project manager a detailed picture of all activities in the project. The project plan is an essential component to the project manager's arsenal of tools. It is central in planning and tracking. In fact, the project plan itself is a repository for most task detail, including resource assignments, planned accomplishments, completed accomplishments, plus numerous other critical data, including dependencies between various tasks. In addition, project plans provide an excellent overview of the project effort including milestones, identifying the critical path, and identifying available float in the schedule. We will discuss critical path and float more later. The project information is summarized in a variety of ways including milestone reports and *Gantt* charts. Project plans and project management software are fairly standardized in terms of basic features and expectations. As a project manager, you will want to become very comfortable with your plan.

ONE WAY THAT WE KEEP EVERYONE FOCUSED ON OUR PROJECT'S OBJECTIVES IS BY SPEAKING IN TERMS OF SPECIFIC MEASURABLE THINGS

Things you can measure

A milestone chart is a report that depicts where in the project the milestones are scheduled. A Gantt chart is a graph of work packages or tasks depicting start and end dates, planned overlaps in tasks as they run in parallel, and illustrating dependencies. Most project management software provides the capability for these various views of the project.

One way that we keep everyone focused on our project's objectives is by speaking in terms of specific, measurable things. Your conversation and your reporting should be oriented this way. One prime example is using milestones. What is a *milestone*? PMI® says this, "A milestone is a significant point or event in a project, program, or portfolio."[xv] You need some significant points or events to measure your progress against. This means that early in your planning *as a team* you determine a series of significant points or events to use as benchmarks in the life of the project. Remember that this is not an activity to be done in isolation. You need your team. They not only have valuable input for you, but if they are part of the process to create the milestones, they will more readily own the milestones as their own, if they played a part in creating them. They will have *buy-in* to the milestones.

A complementary structure frequently used in parallel with milestones or integrated into them is the concept of *gates*. Many organizations establish a standard sequence through which all projects move. The project passes through a series of gates. For example, think of our earlier discussion about the project management process. We called out five phases: Initiating, Planning, Executing, Monitoring and Controlling, and Closing. These would form natural gates in a project management environment. There are various permutations of these in use today. As projects move through these sequences, they are given heightened attention by senior leadership or awarded increasing levels of funding. In some cases, they mirror the broad stages of the project life cycle, in other cases they employ a sequence that the organization uses more broadly. I think they add healthy structure and a common understanding of how projects are done.

Each of these various perspectives gives the project manager another window from which to challenge his or her assumptions about the project. Each is designed to give insight.

Before we go any further, we need to retrace our steps and address a few terms that I have used along the way – *critical path* and *float*.

In project environments and in the business world generally, people often refer to the critical path. There is often much focus or hand-wringing around this thing called *the critical path*. So, what is it? What do we mean by *critical path*? In a casual sense, people often refer to any action that is essential and core to achieving a shared objective as being *on the critical path*. And this is fine.

ANYTHING DELAYED ON THE CRITICAL PATH WILL DELAY THE PROJECT

However, there is a formal definition for project managers. PMI® defines it as: "The sequence of activities that represents the longest path through the project, which determines the shortest duration."[xvi] Let's think about that. Remember the network diagramming that we talked about earlier. Thinking of the entire project, the critical path is the *longest possible path* through the network with the *shortest duration*. Or stated differently, the path with the greatest number of tasks that takes the least amount of calendar time to complete. In practical terms this means that *anything delayed on the critical path will delay the project*. This is why there is such focus on critical path tasks – any delayed task could delay project completion. Monitoring the critical path is essential for a timely completion of the project. As leaders it is our responsibility to help the team stay focused on this.

Now let's talk about *float*. What is it? Float has several forms. *Free float* is "The amount of time that a schedule activity can be delayed without delaying the early start date of any successor or violating a schedule constraint."[xvii] *Total float* is "The amount of time that a schedule activity can be delayed or extended from its early start date without delaying the project finish date or violating a schedule constraint."[xviii] Another term for float is *slack*. You may also hear this used. But what is *float* or *slack*? When I have all of my tasks arranged in a network configuration, some tasks are on the critical path and others are not. For those on the critical path there is no buffer, no fluff, no extra time available – there is no float. For those not on the critical path there is some measure of extra time available. We call this available time *float*. And this can vary from wherever you are in the network.

But let's take a moment and appreciate the difference between free float and total float. Free float considers how much time is available between that task in the network and any *successor tasks*. By contrast, total float considers how much time is available between that task in the network and the *end of the project*. Why is this significant? Free float may indicate that you have two days of available time before the next task. Whereas total float may indicate that you have five days of available time before the project end. This tells you that if you *do not* burn up the two days getting to the next task, you will still have five days of available float remaining until the project concludes. However, if you *do* burn those two days, you will only have three days following the next task, of available float until the project end date. It is prudent to maintain as much float as you can along the way to absorb any surprises you may encounter.

One last word on float and critical path. Every project has those tasks that are challenging. Maybe they are just plain difficult and unknown, or a new technology, or some other thing that makes you wonder if you can accomplish it in the planned period of time. Every project has tasks like this. Here's the point, though. Project managers strive – though it is not always possible – to keep those tasks off of the critical path. If they can keep challenging tasks off of the critical path, then those tasks may be able to absorb some available float if they need to. So, working to keep challenging tasks off of the critical path is important, and knowing where you may have float, or available time, is important. These can provide a useful safety net at times.

Grab a few more tools

Now let's add: Change Management, Risk Management, Actions, and Issues Management, Decisions Tracking to the tool box. (No worries. We will summarize all of our tool box essentials in a later section.)

All things change

All things change. In the life of a project this is almost inevitable. The project objectives will change over the life of the project. And because things change, we have a plan to manage that change. Let's go back in our thinking a few steps and remind ourselves that once we established our list of approved requirements, we locked them down. We called them our scope baseline. We said at that time, that the only way to change the scope baseline, or any baseline for that matter, was through *change management*. So, let's look at change management.

Next to controlling your project baselines, there is nothing more important than change management. Why? Because change management controls your project baselines. It is an essential component. Change management is important throughout the life of the project.

If a stakeholder believes that a project baseline needs to be modified, then a change request should be submitted for consideration. Typical examples of this might be a feature added to the final result, or a milestone date changed, or a substantial cost change. Each of these could result in the stakeholder submitting a change request. Let's walk through the change request process.

The change request process

1. A change request is submitted. A change request contains at least the following things:

   - Brief description of change request

   - Estimate of time required to review the change request

   - Approval/rejection of the estimate to review the change request

   - Analysis of impact on the baselines

   - Other factors supporting the change request

   - Approval/rejection of change request

2. Log change request in the change request log

3. Approve/reject the estimate of time to review change request

4. If rejected, log change request disposition in change log

5. If accepted, evaluate impact of change request on the scope cost and schedule

6. Consider other factors

7. Perform a detailed analysis of the revised scope, cost, and schedule

8. Present change request analysis to stakeholders for approval

9. If rejected, log change request disposition in change log

10. If accepted, execute change order through implementation

The change control process involves three forms: Change Log, Change Request, and Change Order.

There are three control points in the process above. First, the approval/rejection to commit time to review the change request proposal. Second, the analysis of the impact of the change request on the existing baselines. And third, the approval/rejection of the change request. We ask the stakeholders if we should commit the time to look more closely at this change. We ask the team - what are the specific impacts to our existing baselines? What is the impact to our current mission? And we ask the stakeholders, given what they know now about the impact to our project objections, would they still want to proceed with the change? Three control points.

Let's imagine that I am walking down a hall and my client sponsor runs up to me, "Hey, look at this! Look at this!" And she thrusts a piece of paper in my face. I quickly look it over and see that it is a change request for a very minor thing. "How long will this take? How long will this take?" she presses me.

I say, "Oh, just 2 hours at the most. Nothing more... just two hours."

She says, "Hey, thanks..." and she runs off down the hall.

But let's compare that to another scenario. Again, I am

walking down the hall and my client sponsor runs up to me, "Hey, look at this! Look at this!" And she thrusts a pile of papers in my face. I gasp and grab hold of the weighty stack of documents and see that it involves a complex technical change to our plans. "How long will this take? How long will this take?" she barks at me.

I say, "Oh, wow! Just a minute here. I'm going to have one of our technical staff look this over. This is pretty involved and complex. It will likely take us two weeks to review this document and get back to you. Is that OK?"

She says, "Two weeks!? No, no. I don't want to spend the money. Thanks anyway..." and she grabs her papers and runs off down the hall.

Two different scenarios. Two different kinds of estimates, two very different levels of complexity. In the first instance, my initial review or *sizing* of the proposed change took me only a moment's time. But the second situation would take me two weeks to assess the size and magnitude of the change.

Analyzing change requests often falls to those on the team with the most experience. This means that your most valuable - and most limited resources - are the very ones that will be called on to analyze change requests. This explains why we track and account (and often charge) for estimating the size of a change. That *review time is real time, and it can erode our schedule* just as any other unplanned activity can. These activities do have a direct impact on the project schedule and completion date. So, I must control the time. If my key resources are continually evaluating change requests instead of performing the necessary tasks in the project plan, then my project will inevitably be late. So, our stakeholders need to be cognizant of these realities as they consider change requests. Sometimes just reviewing a change directly impacts our project schedule - even if we never accept the change - because reviewing the potential change took valuable resources away from their assigned tasks on the project.

> IF MY KEY RESOURCES ARE CONTINUALLY EVALUATING CHANGE REQUESTS INSTEAD OF PERFORMING THE NECESSARY TASKS IN THE PROJECT PLAN, THEN MY PROJECT WILL INEVITABLY BE LATE

Aware that one of our primary enemies is a subtly expanding scope, we need to press in on several questions. Is the change request important enough to impact our schedule? Is it important enough to alter our expected costs and expand our scope? Are we willing, and is it wise, to alter the definition of what we are doing?

We said that if a stakeholder believed that a project baseline needed to be modified, then a change request should be submitted for consideration. But to whom? That depends. If you and your project are part of a larger enterprise familiar with projects and project management principles, then it is likely that your change request would be submitted to a *change control board* (CCB). The change control board is a group charged with reviewing and approving or rejecting change requests. Who is on the board? Good question. The CCB has a representative group of the broader stakeholder community, representatives from the various aspects of the overall enterprise. And specifically, which parts of the overall enterprise depends wholly on the type of organization it is. For example, a bank would have different areas of interest than a manufacturing company. Who else is on the CCB? The CCB includes a project sponsor signatory, or someone who can sign on behalf of the sponsor. And it includes any project managers with changes up for consideration. In this regard, the project manager is there to promote the change, speak to any questions, and clarify any points about the change request. But what if your organization does not have a CCB? What if your organization is relatively small or simply unfamiliar with project management concepts? In that case, you still want a representative panel to consider these things. Without a CCB how do you do this? Remember, the change control board has three types of members: Project sponsor (or signatory), project manager (with a change request up for consideration), and representative stakeholders from the enterprise (those who can speak to the impact of this change on the organization). What does this tell us? Whether we are talking about a formal CCB or a more informal panel of individuals to review changes, we are always talking about a representative group from our stakeholders. Our stakeholders approved the original three baselines. Now we are saying that any changes to those original baselines must be approved by a representative panel of that same community. Essentially, only stakeholders can change the baselines.

Let's assume for our discussion, that a change request has been approved to the project scope baseline. How does this affect our project baseline? What does it mean that we need to re-baseline? Should we re-baseline our project plan? What does that mean? Do we need to redefine our mission parameters, our points of measurement, in the plan? These are all good questions. Let's look at them.

Every approved change request redefines what it means to be done; redefines what *finished* looks like for the project. So, in a real sense, every approved change request does indeed change our baselines. Yet we don't want to alter what we are aiming at all the time. So, in a practical sense, let's take a closer look at how we use our project *baselines* on a day-to-day basis. Once we have an approved set of requirements and have converted them into workable units, groups of related tasks, or *work packages,* then we further decompose those work packages down into task-level actions. Each task in the project includes at least the numbers of hours of effort and days of duration. Once we have these details, we are ready to *baseline* our project plan. But wait a minute, we already have our three project baselines: scope, cost, and schedule.

What is this baseline of the project plan? Let me explain. On the one hand, we have our three baselines – scope, cost, and schedule. These three carefully define the boundaries of our project effort. They formally demarcate what is included in the bounds of this project and what is not. By contrast, we use a *project plan baseline* to help us measure our progress on the project. This *project plan baseline* is a function or feature available in most project management software applications. Essentially, it *freezes* the scheduled dates along with other data so that ongoing activity can be compared to this fixed position, or baseline, in time.

The project plan baseline is intended to be an *approximate* reflection of the other three baselines. But the primary intention of the project plan baseline is to give us a base to compare against; our progress against a fixed point. Again, what we are aiming at. When the project manager performs a baseline of the project plan, the project management software application captures a fixed image of the project plan expectations at that point. Specifically, it records when every task is scheduled to begin and end, and how much effort and duration has been planned for each. As the project moves forward, current project status is compared to this *baseline*, the fixed image of expectations in the project plan, and the project manager can see if they are on track or falling behind against those expectations. So, the project plan baseline is very important as we manage the project day-by-day but is not a litmus test as to whether something is in or out of scope, as an example. So, you ask, when would we re-baseline a project plan? Under what circumstances? That is up to the discretion of the stakeholders. How so? First, remember that the project plan baselines are *simply a tool for measuring progress*. They are not defining the boundaries of our project in the formal, legitimate way that scope baseline, cost baseline, and schedule baseline define our project. The project plan baseline provides a set point against which to measure to monitor our progress. Consequently, it would not be helpful to re-baseline every time a change request was approved. It would not helpful to the project manager or team comparing the current status against an ever-changing point of reference (the project plan baseline). However, if a major change request is approved; a change request that substantially alters the projects' direction, then the stakeholders must consider whether to re-baseline the project plan. Re-baselining the project occurs when there is significant cost or schedule implications in the change. It is important to involve key stakeholders in the decision to re-baseline. Typically, when a project is re-baselined, a shift occurs in project status reporting, there is a blip in the graphs, or shift in the reporting. Did you notice that this is a decision made by the stakeholders? As in so many things, the project manager never re-baselines in isolation. The project manager would never re-baseline without the full understanding and consent of the stakeholders. Remember, the project plan baseline is used to report project status. It is a key point of reference and has an agreed-upon meaning among stakeholders. So, it is incumbent on the project manager to involve the stakeholders regarding any change in the way project status is gathered and reported. So, re-baselines occur only rarely, and only when a substantial change has occurred on the project.

Life can be risky

What do you think about risk? Part of managing projects is managing the risks around those projects. One thing is clear – risks exist everywhere. Now it is up to us to identify them and manage them to the degree that we can. Risks challenge our project's successful outcome. If we can somehow manage risks, then we can minimize the surprises that will come. This is why we focus on and manage risks - to minimize surprise. So, let's begin.

A risk is "An uncertain event or condition that, if it occurs, has a positive or negative effect on one or more project objectives."[xix]

As the project manager, your world is the project. From the day you launch the project until the day you successfully finish the project, you will manage risks. But how do you identify risks? *Ask*. Begin with your team and move out to your other stakeholders. At the start of your project, ask your team, "What could go wrong on this project?" One thing I have noticed, when you ask someone what could go wrong – there is no shortage of answers. People love to tell us what could go wrong. So, ask your team. And then as the project moves

AS A LEADER, LISTENING IS YOUR PRIMARY TOOL - ALWAYS LISTEN

forward, broaden your inquiry. As a normal agenda item in your status meetings, ask if there are any new risks, or whether any existing risks have become more of a concern. Ask your stakeholders. What is the point? Again, to minimize surprises. Always be open to learning about new or expanding risks. As a leader, listening is your primary tool. Always listen.

As we manage risk, we follow a *risk management process*. This process involves planning, identification, analysis, response planning, and monitoring risks.[xx] It is an iterative process that never ends. It is continuous throughout the project life cycle. Let's simplify this down to three basic pieces – identify, analyze, and control - and go through the process step-by-step.

First, we *identify* risks. We make a list of all risks. This repository or record of risks is called the *risk log*. As we have said, our best source for identifying risks are the people immediately around us; our team and the broader community of stakeholders. Through ongoing inquiry, we keep abreast of new and expanding risks. Specifically, we ask the question, "Are there new or expanding risks?"

Second, we *analyze* risks. What does this mean? Specifically, it means we compare one to the other, and prioritize them. Why? Quite simply, we need to mitigate whatever risks we can. Therefore, we need to invest any time or money into those risks with the highest exposure to affect project success or failure. Let's look more closely at this process. We create our list of all risks. This begins our development of the risk management plan. There are numerous methods and styles available to analyze and prioritize risk. The most important aspect of this discussion is that *we are talking about and weighing the impact of risks* on our project. This is the critical point.

Although there are many approaches to analyzing and managing risk, let's look at one simple example of building a risk management plan that would give us a framework for analyzing and tracking risks. In consultation with our team, we start with a description of the risk. Next, we discuss the *probability* that the risk will happen. Is it a high, medium, or low probability that the risk will occur? If high, let's give it a numeric value of 3.0. If medium, a value of 2.0. If low, a value of 1.0. Next, we discuss the *impact* if the risk does occur. Again, is it a high, medium, or low probability that the risk will occur? If high, let's give it a numeric value of 3.0. If medium, a value of 2.0. If low, a value of 1.0. Then, we discuss what we call the *severity or exposure* to the risk. What is that? It is the combined consideration of impact and probability. Therefore, our severity or exposure to the risk is the product of the impact and probability. We multiply them together to derive the severity or exposure of the risk. For example, a high/high risk would have a severity of 9.0, a medium/medium risk would have a severity of 4.0, and a high/low risk would have a severity of 3.0. When using the simple 1-2-3 scale, I often include one position to the right of the decimal point. I do this because as we are working with these situations each day, we can usually see that although two risks may be medium, generally speaking, one or the other has some aspects that make it a little bit more of a risk than the other. The additional decimal point allows for subtleties and nuance between various risk situations. Ultimately, the severity or exposure value will be used to prioritize the risks. Once we have considered each risk in this way, we will sort our list on the severity value, highest to lowest. This will cause our highest exposure risks to float to the top of the list and give the greatest visibility to our "bad boy" risks. These high exposure risks are where we should focus any available time or money in mitigation.

But before we go any further, the team should establish a *risk response strategy* for each risk. What is that? Essentially, it is a preliminary strategy decision in the event that this risk presents itself. This does not have to be complicated. For example, if I have a low impact/low probability risk I may elect to simply *accept* the risk exposure. Accept would be my strategy in this case. On the other hand, if your team decides to set aside funds in the event that the risk becomes a reality, we would say that you have set up a *reserve* in the event of the risk. But what if you have considered the risk situation, and have developed a fallback plan, a supplementary plan, to invoke in the event of the risk. In such a situation, we would say that you have a plan to

THE MOST CRITICAL ELEMENT IN ALL OF THIS IS SIMPLY THAT WE ARE TALKING ABOUT AND COGNIZANT OF THE RISKS

mitigate the risk in the event of the risk occurring. These are the main risk response strategies used. Your organization may have others. Your process may involve greater or lesser detail. But again, the most critical element in all of this is simply that *we are talking about and cognizant of the risks* that are among us. And we are making plans in the event of risks occurring.

Lastly, we *control* risks. This means that we are tracking and reacting to our risks. As we continue with the risk management process we track our risks. We regularly and systematically revisit our risk management plan and update it. As a team and as a stakeholder community, we ask if any risks have fallen off of the list. Have risk probabilities or impact changed? Have we shifted our response strategies in any way? Or, are there new or expanded concerns? To track risks means that we regularly - typically weekly and monthly - ask all of these types of questions. It means that we frequently poll our stakeholders for new risk exposures. As project managers and leaders, we need the combined insights of everyone in order to successfully achieve our project's objectives. And when a risk presents itself, we *react* to it. Risks do occur. Risks do materialize and become reality.

Our reaction to the risks occurring is our risk response strategy. Remember, we have already determined what to do in the event of the risk. What did we decide to do? We execute the strategy we have already decided on as a team. Good leadership is characterized by minimizing surprises. Our reaction to materialized risks highlights this truth. Although we hope to minimize and avoid as many risks as we can, when they do occur, we have a plan. We are not surprised. We simply execute our predetermined strategy and move on.

Let's summarize our approach to managing risk. We accomplish this in a transparent environment where risks are discussed and explored openly; where every stakeholder has the freedom, and in fact responsibility, to raise any valid concerns regarding the project. Our risk management strategy is our on-going risk dialogue in our status meetings and elsewhere. As we explore risks, we iteratively move each risk through identifying, analyzing, and controlling. In this manner, we manage our risks.

When we talk about risks, we are discussing when things do not go as planned. In project management we set aside funding in the event things do not go as planned. Looking back at our previous discussion, when we analyzed our risks we said that we could potentially set aside funding should the risk present itself. This is formally called a *contingency reserve*. When project teams establish their project budget, one of the things they look at is how much contingency to allow or set aside for the entire project effort. In practical terms, once the team has completed their bottom-up estimate, the contingency percentage is calculated based on the bottom-up estimate and added to the overall project budget. This is one of the *levers* in our project budget. We can nudge the budget in allowance of our risks. A common value is to set aside 10% of the overall budget for a contingency reserve. Some enterprises have an established percentage to use. At times, given the level of complexity or other considerations, an enterprise may establish a greater or lesser percentage. It is good stewardship of the project to acknowledge that things do not go as planned and that we need to make an allowance for this through a contingency reserve.

Before we leave our risk discussion, let's consider one final aspect. Imagine you are the designated project manager over a project that is in pre-launch. You are involved in all of the discussions about the project. In fact, you've probably even roughed-in an initial project plan, helped others establish some top-down, high-level estimates for the proposed project, and been involved in the detailed discussions of what is expected in the effort. My question to you is – how do you *feel* about this overall project? You've been involved in all the details. So, how do you *feel* about it? Are you feeling good about this, or does it make you uncomfortable? What is your *sense* of it? Based on your experience as a project manager and on what you have seen to date regarding this project, you have an impression of how it will go. What is your confidence about the project success or failure? This *confidence level* is another of the *levers* in our project budget. Given your sense of the effort as the project manager, you introduce a *confidence ratio* or percentage to the project budget.

Some things are just part of life

Sometimes people think that *issues* are bad things and that we should avoid discussing them. Some believe that issues are evidence of a broken process or dysfunctional situation, an admission of some failure of leadership on our part. Not necessarily. But here is the plain reality - issues exist. They exist whether a process is broken or not. They exist whether a situation is dysfunctional or not. It doesn't matter if we refuse to see them, they are there. Issues exist and they must be addressed face-on and directly. The truth is that issues are just part of life. And, important to our discussions at the moment, they are part of the everyday life on a project. Issues come up. So, we must address them. In a similar way, *actions* are taken on a project for one reason or another. The team may have questions or points of inquiry. They may need to look into some aspect of the environment to confirm a direction of the project. Whatever the situation, actions are assigned and taken. We call these things *actions and issues management*. Every project manager needs to manage issues and actions. It is an ongoing activity that begins with the start of the project and runs until the project is complete.

Let's look at *issues and actions management*.

First, what is an *issue*? PMI® defines an issue as, "A point or matter in question or in dispute, or a point or matter that is not settled and is under discussion or over

which there are opposing views or disagreements."[xxi]
Experientially these are often the spawning ground for
new risks. So, we keep a special eye on them. As issues
are raised, they are added to the issue log and tracked.
This repository or record of key issues is called the *issue
log*. Their status is discussed each week and revised
accordingly. Each issue log entry would typically
include: Issue identifier number, short description, issue
consequence (for example, schedule slippage), priority
(for example Low/Medium/High, or alternatively
1.0/2.0/3.0), date raised whom, raised by, issue owner,
target date for resolution, status (open, assigned, or
closed), status date, and any additional comments. Each
issue would be individually listed and tracked.

Second, what is an *action*? An action is a thing done, an
act on behalf of the project, which the team feels there is
a significant reason to track. We don't track every action,
of course, only those that have special influence or
significance to the team or the project. As actions are
raised, they are added to an action log and tracked. This
repository or record of key actions is called the *action
log*. Their status is discussed each week and revised
accordingly. Each action log entry would typically
include: Action identifier number, short description,
priority (for example Low/Medium/High, or
alternatively 1.0/2.0/3.0), action owner, date assigned,
target date for current activity, date launched, date
completed, status (open, assigned, or closed), associated
action/issue ids (if this action is related to other issues or
actions), and any additional comments. Each action
would be individually listed and tracked.

Actions and issues management is intended to encourage

an open and honest environment on the project. We talk about things so that we can understand and resolve things before they become significant problems.

Now let's look at *decisions tracking*. Similar to actions and issues, we don't track every decision. However, we should track and maintain a log of any decision for which the team feels there is a strong reason to track. This repository or record of key decisions is called the *decision log*. Again, we don't track every decision, but if there is special significance or influence to the team or the project, we need a record of it. Each decision is individually listed and tracked.

The risks, actions, issues, and decisions logs are often combined into a single spreadsheet workbook with tabs for each log – risks, actions, issues, decisions. This is the Project Logs Workbook.

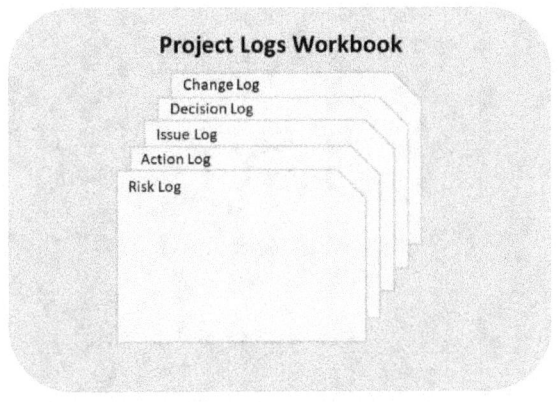

These are sometimes referred to as the RAID logs. For convenience, consider maintaining the project *change log* in the same workbook. In my work, I prefer to save a fresh copy of these logs using the week-ending date of the current week, so that by week's end, I have a complete set of current logs for the week. The following week, I capture a new copy using next week's ending date and repeat the process. In this manner I have a record – *by week* – of the various logs, should I ever need to refer back to a particular week to address some question or review some past situation. This can be invaluable at times. (By the way, I use filenames with dates embedded even when the environment includes a repository structure such as Sharepoint. This convention has served me well.)

Part 4

Manage and execute the project

Let's think of our project as a road trip. We have our destination, a roadmap and guidebooks, the conversation among the travelers, an odometer, the dashboard, and the binoculars. All of these things give us the tools we need to make it an enjoyable trip and bring us successfully to our destination. We will look at each one.

Our destination

In our road trip analogy, the destination is certainly our project objective, our mission. Let's make the point here that our destination must be clear and precise: no ambiguities about where we are going. As we have said, the project charter includes a high-level statement about where we are headed that formally brings the project into existence and gives the project manager authority to lead. It may be helpful to provide a *project scope* definition for further clarity.

> The project scope statement is the description of the project scope, major deliverables, assumptions, and constraints. The project scope statement documents the entire scope, including project and product scope. It describes, in detail, the project's deliverables and the work required to create those deliverables. It also provides a

common understanding of the project scope among project stakeholders. It may contain explicit scope exclusions that can assist in managing stakeholder expectations. It enables the project team to perform more detailed planning, guides the project team's work during execution, and provides the baseline for evaluating whether requests for changes or additional work are contained within or outside the project's boundaries.[xxii]

Also, we have seen that the requirements analysis, the breakdown process, and establishment of our baselines helped us to translate our original objectives into much lower-level, doable kinds of things, tasks that in the broad aggregation are equivalent to our high-level project objectives. In the end, we are left with a set of clear and precise objectives expressed in the form of tasks to be accomplished. So, we know where we are going. We are pointed in the right direction, and we have a clear concept of our destination, our goal. But how do we stay on course?

A roadmap, guidebooks, and signs

The way we stay on course is by using a roadmap and studying the guidebooks. The roadmap is our project plan and the guidebooks include our approach, our processes and methodology, our tools. Now we have added change management, risk management, actions and issues management, or decisions tracking helping us as signs along the way. We use the project plan to map our way to the project's destination. We use the methodology and processes to help us to appreciate our surroundings with more understanding. And we have signs to advise us if we are on course.

The conversation among the travelers

Any road trip where we are traveling in the company of others involves conversation. What is the content of our conversations? This includes our stakeholder relationships. Is our conversation encouraging the team toward our project's objectives, supporting them with helpful insights, or is life on the project simply burdensome? Is it viewed as unpleasant and difficult, or are people truly jazzed to be a part of the endeavor?

DO OUR PEOPLE COME AWAY FROM CONVERSATIONS WITH A FRESH PERSPECTIVE? DO THEY COME AWAY INSPIRED TO DO AMAZING, STARTLING, WONDERFUL THINGS?

As we said earlier, the project manager's primary role is one of inspiring and motivating the team and stakeholders. Do our people come away from conversations with a fresh perspective? *Do they come away inspired to do amazing, startling, wonderful things?* I hope so. As leaders, this is our most important responsibility.

An odometer

On road trips we like to track our miles. We like to know how far we have come toward our goal. And if the journey is quite long, we may even break it down, and watch the miles click off in increments of 100 miles at a time, or distance to the next town. We like to measure our progress. Projects are the same. The odometer in our road trip analogy includes our status meetings and our status reporting. These are methods of communicating our progress against our project's objective. The status meetings and reporting provide the means of measuring our progress against the end goals. Not only that, they provide the project manager and the team with enough information to celebrate even the little wins along the way. Are we using our status meetings in this way? We should. As we said earlier, the status meetings and status reporting are two of the principal means that a project manager has to tell the good story of the project, to keep the team focused, to herald the successes and to provide cautionary words about potential risks. Status meetings are the regular avenue for the project manager to encourage the team. Are we building our relationships or tearing them down? Are we encouraging each other toward our project's objectives, supporting each other with helpful insights, or is everything simply a problem, and viewed as unnecessary reporting?

Do our people come away inspired to do great work, to innovate and think creatively? This is the goal. As leaders, it is our responsibility to foster a motivational atmosphere on our projects.

The dashboard

When traveling on a road trip, it is always prudent to keep your eye on the dashboard. It can alert you if a mechanical condition is threatening your trip's advance. It can advise you of your forward speed, oil pressure, battery health, and even sometimes the external temperature and weather conditions. Basically, it gives you a snapshot of the condition of your vehicle and of the immediate environment to help you make wise decisions along the route. On projects it is also prudent to have a dashboard - a snapshot of the overall condition of the project with information about any pertinent environmental conditions that may affect your project's forward progress. Project dashboards include *key performance indicators* (KPIs) monitoring how we are performing against scope, cost, schedule, and quality. These may be in the form of numeric readouts, or the use of a simple stoplight approach. Organizations will elect to track a selected number of these to see how a project is progressing against its goal.

There are many fine examples of KPIs on the Internet. Many are integrated with an organization's broader systems. Others not. Some, are updated dynamically, given their integrated design, while others are manually maintained. Dashboards provide a summary snapshot of the state of the project, or all projects, at a point in time. They often include a summary of the project milestones or gates achieved to give us a sense of where we are on the project. They give us a status read of the project. Are the milestones coming in on time, or are they delayed? Much of this is *quantitative* in nature.

In some examples, the dashboard looks at other *qualitative* aspects, various dimensions of the project. I think this is vital. For example, you may decide that your dashboard will include indicators of whether the scope is under control or whether the team is committed, and perhaps other dimensions, as well. For each dimension, you and your team would discuss the state of health for each dimension. And you would assign a *state of health* symbol to each of the dimensions. Some organizations use the basic symbols *red* (requiring immediate attention, urgent), *yellow* (requiring attention, but not urgent), and *green* (no extraordinary attention required, maintain current activities). Notice what is happening here. We are asking our team and other stakeholders to *give us a sense* of how various aspects of the project environment are working. We are seeking to understand the *underlying atmosphere or spirit* among those involved on the project. You may be asking yourself why we are interested in *the team's sense of things* when we have a number of quantifiable

EXTRAORDINARY PROJECT OUTCOMES ARE DRIVEN BY THE HEART OF THE TEAM AND NURTURED BY THE LEADER

measures to track our progress. The reason is simply this. Extraordinary project outcomes are *driven by the heart of the team* and nurtured by the leader. Oftentimes the team has an intuitive sense about things like risks, actions, issues, decisions, and the like. They have a sense of positive or negative outcomes. If we want extraordinary outcomes and extraordinary teams, we need to be listening.

As you think about your own dashboard, keep it simple. The idea here is *to give you and others – stakeholders, executives, whoever -* a simple way to keep your fingers on the pulse of the project. Given these key dimensions of the project, we are asking simply, "How are we doing?" Keep things lean by having at most ten, and preferably fewer. I recommend six or seven. Our purpose in this is to *get a read* on the atmosphere of the project. Is the environment healthy? Are people valued and encouraged, are they given the freedom to innovate and amaze? You can't know these things definitively, but you can put your finger in the air periodically and get a sense of the climate on the project. Here are a few dimensions to consider including:

- Mission – Are the team and stakeholders focused on the project objective?

- Team – Are the team and stakeholders given the freedom to perform? Are the team and stakeholder interactions healthy?

- Scope – Is there a clear understanding of the project requirements, what is in scope and what is out of scope? Is there agreement?

- Cost – Is there a clear understanding of the cost or budget for the project? Is there agreement?

- Schedule – Is there a clear understanding on the schedule, milestones, and end date? Is there agreement?

- Risk – Are all risks being discussed, tracked, and addressed? Are any ignored or hidden?

- Change – Is change management the only means of altering project scope? Is it an effective control on scope creep? Are all changes following the change management process?

- Issues - Are all issues being discussed, tracked,

and addressed? Are any ignored or hidden?

- Communication – Are we communicating effectively? Do all stakeholders feel they have the information they need? Does anyone feel out of the loop or ignored?

Numerous other dimensions could be called out. The question is – what is important to your organization, what is critical to monitor?

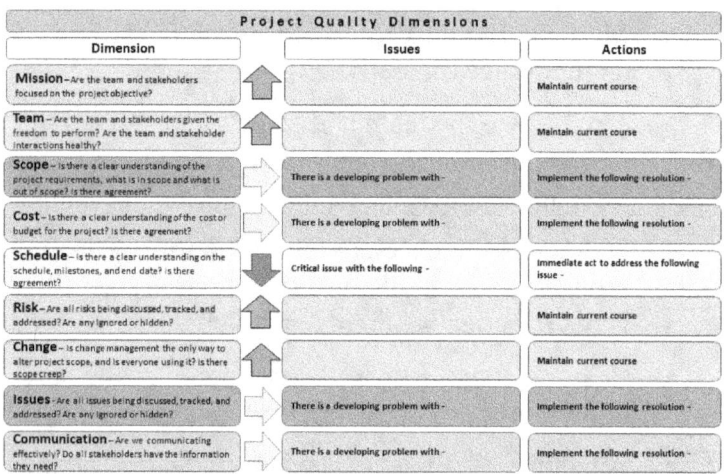

Project Quality Dimensions

Dimension	Issues	Actions
Mission – Are the team and stakeholders focused on the project objective?		Maintain current course
Team – Are the team and stakeholders given the freedom to perform? Are the team and stakeholder interactions healthy?		Maintain current course
Scope – Is there a clear understanding of the project requirements, what is in scope and what is out of scope? Is there agreement?	There is a developing problem with -	Implement the following resolution -
Cost – Is there a clear understanding of the cost or budget for the project? Is there agreement?	There is a developing problem with -	Implement the following resolution -
Schedule – Is there a clear understanding on the schedule, milestones, and end date? Is there agreement?	Critical issue with the following -	Immediate act to address the following issue -
Risk – Are all risks being discussed, tracked, and addressed? Are any ignored or hidden?		Maintain current course
Change – Is change management the only way to alter project scope, and is everyone using it? Is there scope creep?		Maintain current course
Issues – Are all issues being discussed, tracked, and addressed? Are any ignored or hidden?	There is a developing problem with -	Implement the following resolution -
Communication – Are we communicating effectively? Do all stakeholders have the information they need?	There is a developing problem with -	Implement the following resolution -

Other dashboard styles may include an analysis of the overall portfolio of projects with percentages of projects at launch, design, development, build, deploy, or whatever stages of project phases you wish to use. They may give measures of milestones delivered on time, currently on schedule, or late. And the dashboard may allow the viewer to *drill down into* those projects that are late; to see which they are, why they are late, and what can be done to remedy the situation. Dashboards are for all to see. The choices are innumerable. Dashboards are intended to provide a quick analysis of the health of the project environment. These can be print only, but are often on-line displays, many with real time status. The important thing is that the dashboard is a basic communication tool. Therefore, ease of use and simplicity are vital. It is important to keep the approach simple and straight-forward so that the greatest number of people can benefit from using it.

The best example of a dashboard that I have ever seen belonged to a client of mine. The dashboard included a number of summarized data regarding projects. One aspect was a summary of all projects categorized by green/yellow/red status. The definitions of the colors were defined by the client and went as follows. Green was a healthy project. Yellow needed some attention but was moving along. Red were those projects in jeopardy, facing serious challenge of one kind or another. The dashboard provided the ability to drill down into the details behind the summary numbers. So, anyone with access to the dashboard could drill down into the red status projects (or any projects for that matter) to see which ones they were, and what the issues might be. Here is the amazing thing. The individual overseeing all of the projects, the very person who had designed and implemented the dashboard and other features, had also taught and encouraged the senior management at the company how to effectively use the dashboard. To take a quick review

NOT TO LOOK FOR PROBLEMS AND FIND FAULT, BUT ASK WHAT THEY COULD DO TO HELP of the project dashboard each day with the express purpose to look for specific projects in crisis. But more than this, the senior executives were encouraged *not to look for problems and find fault*, but to *ask what they could do to help* find a solution. The senior executives were taught to ask a simple question, "What can I as a senior executive do to help you get your project on track?" The dashboard and the overall project oversight was very successful. Amazing results. This is true leadership at work.

The binoculars

Wouldn't you love to see into the future? And if you think about our road trip, wouldn't it be helpful to know if you will end your journey with a few dollars in your pocket, or if you will run out of fuel a few miles short of your destination? Wouldn't it be nice to know where you are going to end up? Let me make a

GIVEN YOUR CURRENT TRAJECTORY, WHERE WILL YOU END UP?

suggestion. Lean your head out of the window and look through your binoculars at the road ahead. Do you see it there? Or perhaps this is the vehicle *savnat* system. Off in the distance you can see the end of our journey. It is always comforting to know where you are headed, especially on a road trip. But, again, projects are no different than our road trip. Project managers often wish they could see into the future, and they certainly want to know where they are going. So, let me give you some really big news. You *can* see into the future. Well... not exactly. But you can see – *given your current trajectory*

– where you will be at the project's endpoint. *You have headlights into the future!* There is a way to answer the simple question – given your current trajectory, where will you end up. You don't have to wonder and speculate anymore. You can know exactly where you will end up. But it gets even better. Wouldn't it be great if you discovered, when you were only about 25% into the project, that you were over budget or behind schedule? If you are way off track, you would have time to correct any errors and move on. Regardless of when you discover that you are off-track or headed in the wrong direction, with your binoculars in hand you have some time to fix the problems. But what is all this about binoculars?

Remember, projects are like our road trip. We have maps and guidebooks, but we also have ways of seeing into the distance and traveling in unknown territory.

When I speak about *headlights into the future* and having *binoculars*, I am speaking of *earned value* and *earned value measurements (EVM)*. Earned value measurements are some of the coolest tools in the project manager's arsenal. I use images like headlights into the future and binoculars because they accurately depict the role of these tools in the project manager's experience. They are simply amazing tools. Let's have a closer look.

Headlights into the future

Earned value calculations and measurements seem overwhelming at first. But let me gradually tell the story, and I think they will become clear very quickly.

What are earned value measurements (EVMs)? They are

a collection of indices and ratios derived from four values related to project activities. These are the four values: planned value, actual cost, earned value, and budget at completion. The derivative indices and ratios that comprise EVMs provide valuable analysis about the state of the project relative to budgeting and scheduling, and overall completion. But we must have these four values in order to calculate EVMs. Once we have these values, earned value calculations are available to us to help us manage the project. Now let us look at each of the four values to better understand their meaning.

Planned Value – *Planned value (PV)* was formerly called the budgeted cost of the work scheduled (BCWS). If we were to follow the PV from the beginning of the project through to the end, we would discover that when the PV has been exhausted, or fully used, it is equal to the *budget at completion (BAC),* or quite simply, the project budget. By the way, if the PV were plotted on a chart depicting the life of the project from beginning to the end, we would see the entire curved slope of the PV from the project start to the finish. This is because we plan how we are going to spend the budget early in the life of the project. And if I stop at any point along the way in the progress of the project, say three weeks into the effort, I would find the *cumulative* PV for that *point in time;* namely, I would find the PV for three weeks into the project. What does this tell us? It tells us that the PV is *nothing more or less than the planned release of my project budget.* It answers the question: When do we spend the budget?

Actual Cost – *Actual Cost (AC)* was formerly called the actual cost of the work performed (ACWP). The AC, like the PV is a cumulative, point-in-time value for the project. Unlike the PV, though, we can only know the values up through the current point in time. The actual cost is quite simply – actual cost. It answers the question: What have we spent?

Earned Value – *Earned value (EV)* was formerly called the budgeted cost of the work performed (BCWP). What is it exactly? Well, unfortunately, people disagree. They don't disagree on *what* it is, but they disagree on *when* you can declare it. Some people say that you cannot declare earned value until the project is complete, or the phase is done, or the activity is complete, or the milestone is accomplished, or the task is complete. Essentially, there is disagreement *when* to declare it. So, what is it? "Earned value (EV) is a measure of work performed expressed in terms of the budget authorized for that work."[xxiii]

Budget at Completion – *Budget at completion (BAC)* is nothing more complicated than the overall project budget. At the end of the project, it is the sum of all planned value.

So, if your organization has a policy, follow it. But if not, keep things simple. How do we keep it simple? When you are calculating EV, declare it *for the project as a whole*. Although you (or your project management software) have the wherewithal to calculate EV on a task-by-task level, I have never seen the value in it. At that level there is too much investment in details that are not useful in *leading* a project. On the other hand, monitoring and tracking the EV at a project level is of immeasurable value. With earned value I am able to keep my project headed in a direction that is consistent with our original plan. Using EVMs, there will be no surprises in the budget or schedule. In fact, with EVMs I can even see them coming well in advance and take corrective actions before the project is even at risk. There is enormous leadership strength in all of this.

In my own experience, I have typically been the one telling others about earned value and educating them on how it benefits project managers and executives to achieve their project objectives with success. I have been told such things as, "Wow! I didn't realize that project managers had such *cool tools*." And these comments have come from senior executives. The earned value tool is straight forward and powerful.

So, let's keep it simple. The simplest formula for earned value is $EV = BAC * percent\ complete$

What other components do you need? What is necessary for you to calculate and benefit from earned value and EVMs on a regular basis? You will need the percentage complete on the project. Time to grab the project plan.

First, you need your completed project plan detailing each task with resource assignments. This will be periodically updated with the *percentage complete* on each task, and for the project as a whole. Your team reports a percentage complete for the tasks they are assigned, and you or your staff record these values. Once the detailed tasks have been periodically updated, you will use the overall aggregated project percentage available in your project plan to complete your EV calculations.

Second, you will need a structure to hold your planned

value. Think of a spreadsheet with rows and columns. Each row is a specific planned resource, a person, a team member. Each column is a specific increment of time, such as a week or a month. Each cell contains the hours for the period for the person. (I prefer increments of weeks.) Also, include the hourly rate for each resource. For simplicity, I use often use a *blended rate* for all resources. A blended rate is essentially an average rate for all resources. Early in the project planning, you and the team need to think through when each resource will be needed, and how much time will be required at what hourly rate. Be sure to allocate all of your budget. This represents your *budget at completion (BAC)*. Now you have your *planned value (PV)*, and it runs from the beginning to the end of the project. In fact, you could chart your planned spend of the project budget on a line graph.

Third, capture your actual cost for the period. How many hours did each resource work at what hourly rate? The accumulated value is AC. Now you have your *actual cost (AC)*. You could chart your actual costs-by-period up through the present on the same graph as you did with the planned value.

Fourth, calculate your earned value.

$$EV = (BAC) * percent\ complete$$

And again, you could chart your earned value on the same graph as planned value and actual cost.

By the way, the line graph that depicts budget at completion, planned value, actual cost, and earned value is a classic earned value management tool. This should be in your arsenal. (see appendix)

	Start	Month01	Month02	Month03	Month04	Month05	Month06	Month07	Month08	Month09	Month10	Month11	Month12
Planned Value by Month	12000	84000	144000	244000	324000	424000	484000	584000	664000	744000	844000	924000	1000000
Actual Cost by Month	11000	63000	115000										
Earned Value by Month	20000	50000	90000										

So, your question might be: What does a healthy project look like on such a graph? A healthy project is one where you see that the actual cost and earned value *weave in and around the planned value curve*; and they maintain a fairly close tolerance, or proximity, to the planned value line. What indicator tells me that my project is off track and heading for trouble? The warning sign is when you observe that the earned value line is trending away from the planned value line over the course of several periods. If you do observe this trend, in all likelihood you are also aware of circumstances on the project that are contributing to it. The earned value analysis is your wake-up call that a situation has aggregated to a dangerous level. It also gives you the information, the data that you need, to go to your executives and stakeholders and say, "We have a problem here, and I need your help. Together, we can handle this. Together, we can pull this project back on plan. We can get our earned value back in line with our plan, back where we want it." The EV analysis gives you, the project manager, the quantitative data, the facts and numbers you need to engage the broader community to get the project back where it needs to be.

This is only the first level of earned value analysis. We can observe trends in the projects, and these can be helpful. But let's go a little deeper and see what other analysis is available.

As we said, EVMs are a collection of indices and ratios that are derived from the four values we have been talking about. EVM analysis provides insight about the *current state* of our project, and the *future state* of the project based on the project *trajectory;* that is to say, our current direction.

Let's take out our binoculars are see where we are headed. Here are a few examples.

Schedule variance and schedule performance index

When we think about schedule variance, let's begin with what PMI® says about it.

> Schedule variance (SV) is a measure of schedule performance expressed as the difference between the earned value and the planned value. It is the amount by which the project is ahead or behind the planned delivery date, at a given point in time. It is a measure of schedule performance on a project. It is equal to the earned value (EV) minus the planned value (PV). The EVM schedule variance is a useful metric in that it can indicate when a project is falling behind or is ahead of its baseline schedule. The EVM schedule variance will ultimately equal zero when the project is completed because all of the

planned values will have been earned. Schedule variance is best used in conjunction with critical path methodology (CPM) scheduling and risk management. Equation: $SV = EV - PV$[xxiv]

We see, then, that SV is "a measure of schedule performance on a project." In simple terms, how are we doing with our schedule? Are we ahead, behind, or right on target? A positive value indicates that we are ahead of schedule. A negative value indicates that we are behind. And a variance of zero indicates that we are right on the mark. Schedule variance tells us the basic story. At a glance we can see the *state of our schedule*. However, be careful here. A negative value may indicate that we are behind schedule, but that may not necessarily indicate that the project is in trouble. The situation may be understandable given other project contributors. The truth is, if the schedule variance is all we know, then we don't have enough data to make a determination of whether the negative value is good or bad.

Well then, how far off track are we? Whether positive or negative, to what degree are we off? Let's look at the schedule performance index (SPI).

PMI® gives the following description of schedule performance index.

> The schedule performance index (SPI) is a measure of schedule efficiency expressed as the ratio of earned value to planned value. It measures how efficiently the project team is using its time. It is sometimes used in conjunction with the cost performance index (CPI) to forecast the final project completion

estimates. An SPI value less than 1.0 indicates less work was completed than was planned. An SPI greater than 1.0 indicates that more work was completed than was planned. Since the SPI measures all project work, the performance on the critical path also needs to be analyzed to determine whether the project will finish ahead of or behind its planned finish date. The SPI is equal to the ratio of the EV to the PV. Equation: SPI = EV/PV[xxv]

So, the SPI "measures how efficiently the project team is using its time." If we say, for example, that our SPI is 1.06, this indicates that we are ahead of schedule by 6%, operating at 106% efficiency. Or, if we say that our SPI is .89, this indicates that we are behind schedule by 11%, operating at 89% efficiency. And, if we say that our SPI is 1.00, this indicates that we are tight on schedule with a 0% variance on our schedule expectations, operating at 100% efficiency.

Cost variance and cost performance index

When we think about cost variance, let's again begin with what PMI® says about it.

Cost variance (CV) is the amount of budget deficit or surplus at a given point in time, expressed as the difference between earned value and the actual cost. It is a measure of cost performance on a project. It is equal to the earned value (EV) minus the actual cost (AC). The cost variance at the end of the project will be the difference between the budget at completion (BAC) and the actual amount spent. The CV is particularly critical because it indicates the relationship of physical performance to the costs spent. Negative CV is often difficult for the project to recover. Equation: $CV = EV - AC$[xxvi]

We see, then, that CV is "a measure of cost performance on a project." In simple terms, how are we doing with our cost, our budget? Are we over, under, or right on track? A positive value indicates that we are under budget. A negative value indicates that we are over. And a variance of zero indicates that we are right on target. Cost variance tells us the basic story. At a glance we can see the *state of our costs, our budget*. However, again we say, be careful here. A negative value may indicate that we are over budget, but it may not *necessarily* indicate that the project is in trouble. The situation may be understandable given other project contributors. The truth is, if the cost variance is all we know, then we don't have enough data to make a determination if the negative value is good or bad.

So, how far off track are we? Whether positive or negative, to what degree are we off? Let's look at the cost performance index (CPI)?

PMI® gives the following description of schedule performance index.

> The cost performance index (CPI) is a measure of the cost efficiency of budgeted resources, expressed as a ratio of earned value to actual cost. It is considered the most critical EVM metric and measures the cost efficiency for the work completed. A CPI value of less than 1.0 indicates a cost overrun for work completed. A

CPI value greater than 1.0 indicates a cost underrun of performance to date. The CPI is equal to the ratio of the EV to the AC. The indices are useful for determining project status and providing a basis for estimating project cost and schedule outcome. Equation: CPI = EV/AC[xxvii]

So, the CPI "measures the cost efficiency for the work completed." If we say, for example, that our CPI is 1.03, this indicates that we are under budget by 3%, operating at 103% efficiency. Or, if we say that our CPI is .93, this indicates that we are over budget by 7%, operating at 93% efficiency. And, if we say that our CPI is 1.00, this indicates that we are right on budget with a 0% variance on our cost expectations, operating at 100% efficiency.

I said earlier that if my schedule variance or cost variance are negative, it may not indicate that we are in trouble on the project. How so? Let's imagine a scenario. Let's say that in your original plan you had scheduled an expensive resource to come in week eight of the project and perform 40 hours of highly specialized work. Let's assume that their work is necessary for the project, but not dependent on other tasks. Further, let's say that they contacted you in week one and said they had a schedule conflict with your original planned schedule for the work, but that they could come now and complete it. And this is what they did. They completed their work in precisely the allotted time, but not in line with the planned schedule. How will this be reflected relative to cost variance and schedule variance? Cost variance will show a negative impact from the activity – because you have spent more than planned at this time. Schedule variance will show a positive impact from the activity – because you have accomplished more work than planned at this time. In fact, if the work was performed precisely according to plan, the cost and schedule variances will be exact complements of each other. Negative values do not necessarily indicate a problem, but they should cause us to dig into the details to understand what happening. Of course, if both cost and schedule variances are showing negative, this certainly indicates a problem.

To-complete performance index

So far, we have looked at schedule variance (SV) and cost variance (CV) as examples of EVMs available to us and their derivative values SPI and CPI. There are many others. But let me highlight just one more. In additional to the basic schedule and cost variance indicators, the to-complete performance index (TCPI) is perhaps the next most popular and useful of the EVMs. It addresses a basic question. What level of performance is required for my project to finish as planned?

Let's begin with what PMI® says about TCPI.

> The to-complete performance index (TCPI) is a measure of the cost performance that is required to be achieved with the remaining resources in order to meet a specified management goal, expressed as the ratio of the cost to finish the outstanding work to the remaining budget. TCPI is the calculated cost performance index that is achieved on the remaining work to meet a specified management goal, such as the BAC or the EAC. If it becomes obvious that the BAC is no longer viable, the project manager should

consider the forecasted EAC. Once approved, the EAC may replace the BAC in the TCPI calculation. The equation for the TCPI based on the BAC: $(BAC - EV) / (BAC - AC)$[xxviii]

The TCPI "is a measure of the cost performance that is required to be achieved with the remaining resources in order to meet a specified management goal...." Very simply, what performance is required to complete the project as planned? What level of performance will achieve the plan? How hard will the team need to push beyond their estimated effort? In contrast to SPI and CPI, when TCPI values that are greater than 1.00, they are indicating a negative message, whereas values that are less than 1.00 indicate a positive message. Let's look more closely. If we say, for example, that our TCPT is 1.04, this indicates that we must work at 104% of planned performance in order to complete the project as planned. Or, if we say that our TCPI is .87, this indicates that we can work at 87% planned performance in order to complete the project as planned. And, if we say that our TCPT is 1.00, this indicates that we are on target to complete the project as planned.

We have given some considerable thought to EVMs and how they provide insights into our project. *They are headlights into the future.* We use these tools regularly and systematically to guide and manage our projects. But these are not tools just for the project manager alone to play with. We must engage our team members and other stakeholders in the value and usefulness of EVMs. As they appreciate the ways in which we use this tool to help us on projects, we will gain their increased commitment to provide accurate and timely data and their buy-in on levels of performance and effort. EVMs provide a critical base of understanding on the project to all of the stakeholders.

We have covered a lot of ground regarding the financial aspects of a project. The project financials tell a story and give us guidance for the days ahead. So, we need a simple, effective method to maintain our information. In my work, I establish a Project Financial Tracking Workbook - a reasonably simple spreadsheet with multiple tabs covering key areas.

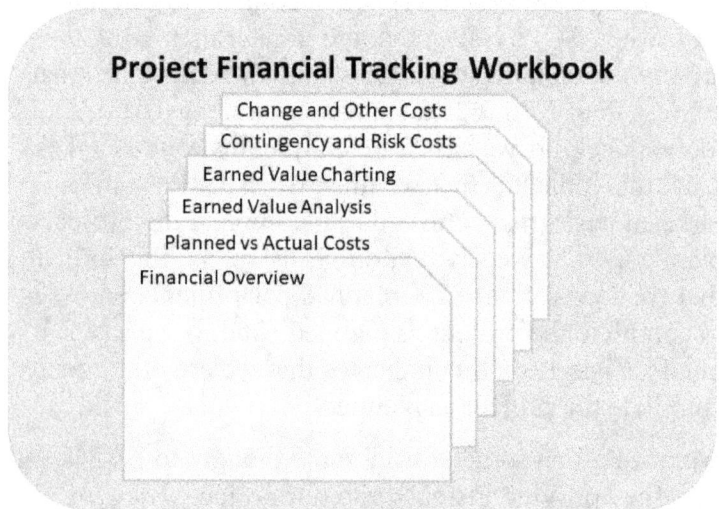

This basic tool provides the means to organize and track planned vs actual costs, earned value analysis and charting, risk and contingency costs, change costs, and other costs. (see appendix)

Checking our maps along the way

As the project progresses along the way, it is important

to pause from time to time to assess where we are. We need to *check our maps* to confirm that we are moving in the right direction at the anticipated speed. This is where status reporting comes in. I recommend that at least two, and sometimes three, regularly scheduled status meetings be used to accomplish this.

First, a *Daily 15 Minute Standup* (yes, it is actually 15 minutes, and you all stand up to keep a spirit of brevity and urgency) is used on many projects. It is sometimes called a *daily scrum* in agile environments. This is an important component especially if the project has a highly compressed schedule. It involves the immediate team and asks only three questions of each member. What did you accomplish yesterday? What are your plans for today? Are there any roadblocks that you need help with? This simple daily formula has been shown to be highly effective in keeping teams moving aggressively toward the objective while giving team members a lot of freedom in the details of their work. For some, a daily meeting is just too much. Whether you use a daily standup or not is driven by the needs of your project and its members.

Second, a *Weekly Status Checkpoint* meeting with your team is a very important component. This is the weekly rallying call to your team to keep them apprised of the overall progress of the effort, and to share with them a sense of how they are contributing to the whole. It is the time to celebrate interim wins and achievements, and to explore those things that did not go well. This meeting includes reporting that becomes a part of the project record. As part of the weekly reporting, I recommend a Milestones and Deliverables Checklist. Let's take a moment and look at it more closely. (see appendix)

The Milestones and Deliverables Checklist is an important tool in your toolbox. This simple tool helps you keep the team highly focused on key progress markers. In all the complexity and detail swirling around projects, this tool keeps everyone's attention on the milestones and deliverables as you lead them to a successful finish.

The Project Milestones and Deliverables Checklist is a compilation of all Milestones, Work Products, Deliverables, and Interlocks for a given project, with a high-level analysis of progress overall.

Before we go any further, let me define each of these four things.

Milestone – A significant event or achievement accomplished on the project
Work Product – A significant output from the team that *is not* designated in the project scope or contractual agreements, produced for the convenience of the team
Deliverable – An output from the team that *is* designated in the project scope or contractual agreements, produced for the benefit of the sponsor or client
Interlock – A critical point-in-time interface with other entities outside of the project where the project may impact or be impacted by the other, or a point-in-time awareness

So, what is the purpose of this checkpoint? To answer that question, let me pose a rhetorical question. How many of you enjoy being in a project status meeting where the project manager methodically plods through the 600 tasks in the project plan each week looking for updates? My guess is that none of you want to be in that meeting. But, honestly, all too often this is how status meetings are conducted – one line, one task at a time. And, yes, most projects have far more than 600 tasks. This approach is just a waste of time and profoundly un-inspiring for the team. This brings us to the purpose be-hind the Milestones and Deliverables Checklist. It was developed to be used with the Weekly Status Checkpoint and the Monthly Status Reporting. It is designed to give a framework for discussion during the weekly and monthly meetings. Its purpose is to keep the team very focused on the project mission – as defined in terms of milestones, deliverables, work products, and interlocks. With the aid of status, a few dates, and a day variance value, we can capture the overall progress of the project almost at a glance.

The information in the Project Milestones and Delivera-bles Checklist gives the project manager the opportunity to celebrate the team's achievements, to acknowledge challenges or slippages the team is facing, and to help the team to sharpen their attentions on the next things. This tool provides the opportunity to support and inspire the team, to recast a fresh vision of the project's mission, and to help those who may be struggling reach even higher. (see appendix)

Third, a *Monthly Status Report* meeting with your executives and sponsors to keep them apprised of project progress. This is a time to share the *significant achievements* of the team and any *current benefits* the organization is enjoying as an outcome of the effort. This is also the time to paint a fresh image of the project objectives, to, once again, cast a vision for what the team is doing, and to call leadership to enthusiastically endorse the team's work toward achieving the organization's goals. (see appendix)

What does 'finished' look like?

In the beginning of the project we began by asking, "What does it mean to be *done*?" We pressed the point with, "What does '*finished*' look like?" As a team, we wanted a clear picture of where we were headed. Progressively, we gained clarity around our mission, making a detailed plan to execute. And as the project progressed, we monitored our focus on our objective. What percentage of the project and what specific things were complete? How close were we to being *done*? In this manner, we have systematically approached *finished*.

It would be unfortunate to reach our end point only to discover that we had missed the mark, that expectations were not met, and essentially, that we had failed. Therefore, it is most important we discuss another aspect of our project – its *quality*. In recent years there has been a heightened attention given to *project quality*. This has been good for everyone involved in these kinds of efforts. My purpose here is to highlight a few project quality elements, and then to paint a couple of broad strokes around the topic. (Much has been written on this lately. I will leave it to the reader to continue their own discoveries.) PMI® defines project quality management as: "Project Quality Management includes the processes and activities of the performing organization's quality policy regarding planning, managing, and controlling project and product requirements, in order to meet stakeholders' expectations."[xxix] It almost goes without saying that a project quality plan would aid in a team's *accuracy* and *precision* resulting in reduced *variation*. These are the things that quality specialists focus on. And with this eye on quality we find increased attention on customer satisfaction, prevention over inspection, continuous improvement, management responsibility, and cost of quality.[xxx]

Looking at *continuous improvement,* for example, PMI® says,

> The PDCA (Plan-Do-Check-Act) cycle is the basis for quality improvement as defined by Shewhart and modified by Deming. In addition, quality improvement initiatives such as Total Quality Management (TQM), Six Sigma, and Lean Six Sigma, could improve the quality of the project's management as well as the quality of the project's product. Commonly used process improvement models include Malcolm Baldrige, Organizational Project Management maturity Model (OPM3®), and Capacity Maturity Model Integration (CMMI®).[xxxi]

Here we find yet other cycles, continuously looping iterations, which help us maintain a healthy project. Keep in mind that we regularly loop, or iterate, through other project aspects all the time. We are always asking about risks, actions, issues, decisions, changes, and so on. We are constantly cycling through these inquiries. Now we add quality to the mix.

If you are using Six Sigma or Lean Six Sigma you will discover this cyclical process further refined as DMAIC, or Define-Measure-Analyze-Improve-Control.[xxxii]

D – Define the goals of improvement activity

M – Measure the existing system

A – Analyze the system to identify ways to eliminate gap between current performance of the system or process and the desired goal

I – Improve the system

C – Control the new system[xxxiii]

DMAIC provides an excellent framework for continuous improvement and control of project quality.

Stay between the lines

Thinking about our road trip, it is important to everyone that we stay between the lines on the road. As we lead our projects we want to do the same – stay between the lines. As we look at project quality, we have tools to aid us in maintaining a steady course. We have upper and lower control limits (UCL/LCL) on project quality.

Not too much to the left or right - just the right direction – the anticipated or planned level of performance. Or think of an aircraft flying at just the right altitude – not too high, not too low. Control charts are one means to help us maintain just the right direction regarding quality. Six Sigma is one option available to you.

To aid us in doing this PMI® highlights seven basic

quality tools: cause-and-effect diagrams, flowcharts, check sheets, Pareto Diagrams, histograms, control charts, and scatter diagrams.[xxxiv]

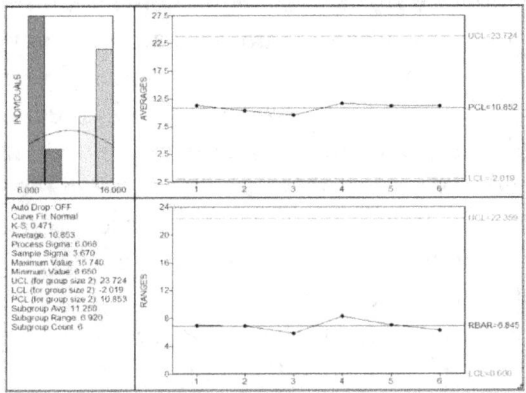

It is easy to appreciate how these will positively impact our project quality in providing a continual corrective lens to our project activities. Whether you are measuring error rates in testing, the rate of user acceptance tests, or the daily velocity of stories in agile, monitoring quality provides added confidence to everyone that the project is focused on a successful mission. I mention these things as a general guideline of some of the options. There are many fine resources available to get into the detailed workings of Six Sigma leadership.

The project has bookends

Earlier we spoke about project life cycles. At that time, we mentioned that we have *starting the project* and *closing the project*. Remember, we said that a project has a defined beginning and an end. We start it and close it. It is worth mentioning these two events before we leave the topic of project execution.

As we have seen, starting the project involves developing a project charter, a communications plan, establishing financial tracking, RAID logs and a change log, selecting the team, establishing checkpoints and status reporting, and much more. In all the flurry of beginning the project, I strongly recommend you begin the formal project with a *Project Kick-Off* meeting. This is typically held once the *project infrastructure* has been established. By project infrastructure I mean the essential project elements are in place such as a charter, communications plan, financial tracking, logs, checkpoints and status, and preliminary project plan. Having a formal Project Kick-Off meeting gives a deeper sense of identity to the project effort, both to the team and the broader community of stakeholders. During this meeting the team is introduced, along with key stakeholders and stakeholder groups. A broad outline of the project mission is given. The project mission is clearly articulated. Other project elements are presented as to how they will be used during the life of the project to achieve the objectives. This is where you begin your focus on the project vision. This is where you begin to generate excitement and spirit for the effort.

In a complementary manner, at the close of a project, it is essential to conduct a *project debrief* meeting with *lessons learned*. Did we accomplish the mission? How did we do? And, most important of all, did we learn anything in the process? This is the time to say, "Thank you" to the team and others, and to celebrate the team's accomplishments. Remember that budget allocation for a celebration party? Use it. This provides formal closure to the project. And with this, the project is complete.

How is all this stuff organized?

Projects involve a fair amount of documentation. Project records form the historic chronicle, may be required in future legal matters, track progress on behalf of leadership, and they provide the means to manage and execute the project. We have discussed a number of these documents in this book. These are only the essential ones that I have found most helpful over the years. I summarize them in the toolbox section. Depending on the nature of the project, you will add more to the mix as you have need. For additional sources of more project management tools and concepts, refer to the bibliography at the back of the book.

Before we go any further, let's discuss where we will keep all of this documentation. We store all of our documents for the project in the *project repository*. In many organizations, all projects and their project managers must follow agreed-upon patterns of storing project documentation in a common manner. It is vital that every project manager maintains their records in the same way. This makes it easy to know where to find the information they need. The repository may exist as a set of folders and files on your laptop, a shared enterprise drive, or a formal system such as a SharePoint environment. What is most critical is that the repository be regularly and systematically backed up. The backup method is most often determined by the organization.

Following project closure, the project repository is permanently stored with other completed projects in the *projects repository*. The projects repository is the compilation of all project repositories following project closure. I strongly *recommend that the projects repository have robust search capability* to allow future project team's the opportunity to review what has been done before. This helps future engagements shape their work to take advantage of the lessons learned, avoid past mistakes, and leverage previous innovations and methods to the benefit of the overall organization. Our project history is one of the best guides in doing future work. It is the record of what we did well, and how we could improve.

What have we got in the toolbox?

I mentioned earlier that I would summarize the essential tools we would need. What should we have inside our project manager's toolbox?

Please refer to the Appendix where I have provided a list of essential document and sample forms.

Part 5

To lead by the fist or by the palm

One of the threads running through this book is that *the way we lead* has a direct impact on the performance of our teams. I have emphasized a number of qualities the leader must have to lead teams to accomplish amazing things. Let's focus on a few in more detail.

You are there to lead the project team to accomplish your project's objectives. True. But the question is – *How* will you do that? Will you bear down on your team in unrelenting pressure until they simply produce the results – one way or the other – or fail in the process? Will you squeeze and squeeze until you get what you want? I mean, you are the boss, right?

WILL YOU DEMONSTRATE TO THEM WHAT IT MEANS TO CARE FOR EACH OTHER BY SHOW ACTS OF KINDNESS AND THOUGHTFULNESS EVEN IN THE STORMS AND PRESSURE OF THE DAY

So, just push and demand what you want. Or is there another way? I think there is. By contrast, will you – even while the pressures swirl around *you*, even while others pound on *you* – will you value your people first, will you encourage them to reach for unexpected and wonderful results, will you demonstrate to them

137

what it means to care for each other by showing acts of kindness and thoughtfulness even in the storms and pressures of the day? If you do the latter, you will be showing them great leadership. You will be encouraging them to their full potential and opening the windows of possibility for your project team to do incredible things. Yes, these things help the overall project effort to reach its goals in startling and amazing ways, beyond expectations. And in the end, in addition to great project results, your people also will have learned more about themselves. They will have grown new skills and come away from the project experience a better, more understanding person.

The things that will have the most powerful impact on your project – and, let's just say, *your life*, for that matter – have nothing to do with numbers or measurements. Nothing at all.

Lead with grace and you will be rewarded beyond measure.

Seeing beyond the sums

One of the dangers in leadership is to rely on counting too much. In our discussions we emphasize the need to speak in specific, measurable terms; namely, numbers. And this is very important. But we must use care on this point to balance our message. It is important that *numbers* are not all we speak about. As project managers, our mission, the project objective, is often defined in terms of numbers; numbers to achieve, numbers to exceed; whether we have achieved our mission or not is measured numerically, Yes, we achieved it, or, no we did not.

> ONE OF THE DANGERS IN LEADERSHIP IS TO RELY ON COUNTING TOO MUCH

Albert Einstein once said, "Not everything that can be counted counts, and not everything that counts can be counted."[xxxv] What does this tell us? On the one hand, numbers themselves are not inherently meaningful. And on the other hand, many things that are meaningful, are not defined by numbers at all. From Einstein's perspective, the universe of the good and useful, the universe of meaningful things, was broader than strictly numeric expression. And we know this from our experience.

If your whole message speaks of numbers, and if your objectives are purely scribed in terms of data points, quotas, and tick points, then the people involved begin to see themselves as only cogs in a wheel grinding work out in raw numeric terms; cold and without consideration for the personal insights or interests of the team or others; just numbers; no sense of deeper purpose or meaning, no sense of the profound or of discovery, only lifeless static numeric expressions. Although we frequently reference our baselines and talk about how we are progressing against them and other measures, the truly important things we have to say to each other have little to do with the numbers. They are all about a deeper, more significant world and experience. And it is on the cusp of these living relationships that truly astonishing results occur, where teams perform extraordinary things.

Leaders and their people

Let me make an observation. As a project manager, you can do all of the things we have discussed in this book *perfectly*, and your projects could still fail. On the other hand, you could do some of these things really *poorly* and your projects could still be very successful. Why? What's the difference? What is that *something* that makes it all come true? As a leader, what do you need to help your people achieve amazing things? How can you serve them best? Here is what I have found in leading people to achieve amazing things.

To Win Their Hearts

What makes a leader someone others will follow? What *something* is it that real leaders have that makes them the kind of person others are drawn to, that others will follow even when the going becomes difficult, or the road is nearly impossible?

I had the unique privilege of traveling the world for ten years conducting classes and workshops for project managers and leaders. My passion was to give them the ability to lead others well. I wove into my talks and presentations the things I have learned in my life. To illustrate how we lead others to achieve incredible results, I drew from my real-world experiences. Both as owner of a software development consulting company and working for one of the largest consulting companies in the world, I saw teams achieve what others thought impossible. Many of my stories centered around my role as an executive project manager for IBM deployed to lead troubled, failing projects back to life, delivering success to both IBM and client.

Management approaches (think project management or quality disciplines as examples) are organized and systematic, and these do position organizations for success. But organization and systematic disciplines are not what bring the success. Some managers are very organized and systematic, yet their efforts fail, while others are not very structured, yet they succeed. Why? The key is the leader. The leader determines success or failure. It is not the bits and pieces of a management approach or discipline. So, the question is - *what is it in the leader that brings the win*?

HAVE YOU CREATED AN ATMOSPHERE THAT DRAWS OTHERS TO WANT TO JOIN THE MAGIC OF YOUR TEAM OR ESCAPE FROM YOUR GROUP?

I used to challenge the people in my classes, "Why should they follow you?" I would ask them, "What makes you so special?" Each of us needs to understand what we bring to the mix and, more importantly, what we lack. Here is a simple litmus test. Have you created an atmosphere that draws others to want to join the magic of your team or to escape from your group? Leaders nurture an atmosphere in which teams thrive and grow, where each person is valued more deeply than the current effort. It is never one person that delivers amazing results. It is the team working in a healthy environment.

So, what do real leaders bring? What qualities are necessary? For me there are only three essential attributes that a successful leader must have.

Speak Truth – A leader must always speak true things. A leader must always speak honestly. He or she must do this even to their own hurt if necessary. Speaking truth is critical to building the trust of those we work with. When others know that we will always be truthful, regardless of the outcome or blowback, they know they can trust us wholly, they can rely on us even under pressure. Leaders begin to build trust by speaking truthfully even in small matters. As I have spoken honestly to clients and teams during hard situations, they have been thankful for an honest word in difficult times. Leaders are living examples of truth-telling, and in this climate, trust grows.

Focus on Mission – A leader must keep his or her people focused on the mission. Does the effort evolve over time? Probably. And when it does, any change must be shepherded carefully so as not to grow exponentially out of control. In this the leader must use great care to keep their people focused on the objective. The leader provides the stabilizing voice. When the team remains focused on the goal, their work organically churns toward the completed objective, obstacles are navigated, and a sense of community develops among those focused on common purpose.

Truly Care – A leader must truly care about the people he or she works with. We often overlook this, but *it is the most critical of all*. If as leaders we simply issue directives and guidelines and expect others to jump on the train, we have missed our primary responsibility as leaders. Our true calling is to inspire: to inspire trust, to inspire to the mission, and to inspire others to accomplish great things. *If we are engaged in anything less, we are not walking as leaders.* Leaders listen and act on behalf of their people. And because we are committed to our people, they will work through impossible scenarios and accomplish incredible things. Our people meet the expectations we set for them. If we expect mediocrity, this is what we receive. If we expect *wonderful*, this is what our people give us. It is a profound joy to be part of a team exceeding expectations and wowing us with their achievements. They accomplish impossible things because we believe they can. I have seen this over and over with situations that seemed unredeemable and completely undoable. Teams will accomplish what is not possible. Believe for the impossible and your people will accomplish the most amazing things.

IN THE END IT IS UP TO US AS LEADERS TO WIN THE HEARTS OF THOSE WE ARE CHARGED TO LEAD

I have shared about speaking truth, focusing on the mission, and caring for our people. In the end it is up to us as leaders to win the hearts of those we are charged to lead. We do this through our words and our actions. Talking with them and getting to know them. Not just how they are contributing to the current situation, but about them as individuals, their own interests and passions. When we intentionally invest in our people and share about things important to each of us, we are touching something deeper than just the current effort. We touch the heart. Here is where real leaders live. We demonstrate that the current struggles are only part of a much larger fabric of relationships that runs deeper than any current difficulty. In this atmosphere people will rise to any challenge and overcome it. And they do this because we have shown that we are committed to them and deeply care about them as people. We have won their hearts.

As leaders we must be authentic. We must speak truth, stay focused on the mission, and truly care about our people. This is how groups of people working together accomplish amazing, startling, wonderful things.

The wisest man in all the world

What qualities make a great leader? How would you know if you had met one? Is there anything to look at as an indication of great leadership? Let me tell you a story.

I arrived in Dalian, China, on 11 October, 2010, in the middle of the night. My luggage had been lost by the airline. I walked up to registration at the Shangri La Hotel and informed the person there that I was checking in. He asked about my travels, and I mentioned my lost luggage.

"Oh!" the hotel desk person said with a surprise, "I have something for you."

I said, "Excuse me. What did you say?"

"I have something for you." And he quickly turned and walked through a doorway behind the reception desk, returning a moment later with a package, handing it to me. "You lost your luggage. We hope this will help you until your luggage arrives."

He immediately presented me with a package of essentials to help me enjoy my stay. This package included a polo shirt with hotel logo, toothbrush, and numerous other things to help me get by until my luggage arrived.

"Thank you very much," I said. This was an unexpected surprise. I thought, "Wow, that was impressive." After checking in, I went to my room. The room was beautiful, restful, and comfortable. I slept until morning.

In the morning, I went down to breakfast. Now things became very interesting. As I entered the lobby, I was immediately greeted by name by hotel staff. They said, "Mr. Lewis, how was your sleep?"

"Fine. Very nice."

"And, Mr. Lewis, would you like breakfast this morning?" I was surprised that they knew my name. I much appreciated their warm and cordial reception.

"Yes," I said, "I would love breakfast." They showed me into the restaurant and handed me over to the hostess and servers. Each person, without exception, showed a personal interest in my experience at the hotel and during my entire stay in Dalian. There seemed to be a perfect balance, providing me information on my choices and experience, yet not becoming intrusive or overbearing. They were focused on providing me with the most pleasant experience. They were there for me. It seemed like it gave them joy to serve others.

Each day, morning and evening, they would stop by my table and engage me in conversation, sometimes to suggest a special dish, other times just to confirm that I was having a wonderful experience at the hotel and in China. I frequented the fitness center, and the staff there were equally devoted to providing a truly memorable experience. As I came to and from the hotel during my stay, I encountered parking attendants and my daily driver. In every situation it was the same. Each person was committed to providing the very best. Most of them knew me by name within a day. Even as I encountered the housekeeping staff, I saw a true commitment to quality and a desire to please the guests. But here is the utterly amazing thing. Everyone working there was smiling. I do not mean that they carried an artificial smile on their faces. Not at all! *Their smiles and the joy they found in serving others was authentic.* It was honest and true and real. As I thought about this, it reminded me of something I had studied in the past.

During much of my career, I have been involved in leadership at many levels. I've led small companies, managed numerous projects – large and small, mentored other leaders, and for a number of years, taught people worldwide how to lead and guide others successfully. I could see that the leadership of the Shangri-La Hotels and, more specifically, the leaders of the hotel in Dalian, had accomplished something that I have never seen. Let me say that again – *they had accomplished something I have never seen, something truly rare* as leaders of people. My experiences at the Shangri-La Hotel in Dalian brought my thoughts back several thousand years.

In 971 - 931 BC there was a great and powerful king named Solomon. He was said to be the wisest man in the world. He was so wise that other reputed wise men would come to him to see for themselves. At one point, the Queen of Sheba, a wise person in her own right, came to test his wisdom with hard questions. She made a startling discovery. Let me quote from an historic record of her encounter.

> Now when the Queen of Sheba heard of the fame of Solomon, she came to Jerusalem to test him with hard questions… And Solomon answered all her questions. There was nothing hidden from

Solomon that he could not explain to her. And when the queen of Sheba had seen the wisdom of Solomon... there was no more breath in her. And she said to the king, "The report was true that I heard in my own land of your words and of your wisdom, but I did not believe the reports until I came and my own eyes had seen it. And behold, half the greatness of your wisdom was not told me; you surpass the report that I heard. Happy are your wives! Happy are these your servants, who continually stand before you and hear your wisdom!^{xxxvi}

What does this historical account have to do with staying at the Shangri-La Hotel in Dalian? It has to do with leaders and leadership. When we think about great leaders and great wisdom, we look to King Solomon as an example. Consider the historical account. First, the Queen of Sheba heard about the wisdom of Solomon, and went to test him, to confirm what she had heard. Second, she saw every aspect of his wisdom - his words, the results of his wisdom in accomplished things, and in his people. In fact, the record is that "the breath went out of her". She was so overwhelmed by his greatness and the wonder of his wisdom that she nearly fainted – it was beyond words. Third, the Queen of Sheba said precisely what quality of his wisdom was so amazing. It was his people. They were happy! His wives, his servants, those who stood before him were happy! This was a most amazing thing!

It was the people's happiness that was such a wonder. The *people's happiness reflected directly upon the wisdom of the leader*, namely Solomon. Achieving true happiness in people requires wisdom from the leader. It is rarely achieved. Rarely. At the Shangri-La Hotel in Dalian, I saw with my own eyes that every housekeeping person, every parking attendant, every driver, hostess, every registration person, every manager, every person reflected an authentic happiness. *Every person was truly happy.* This made every guest feel at ease, comfortable, and valued. It assured the highest quality from staff and the most rewarding experience for the guests. This happiness created a peaceful, almost therapeutic, healing atmosphere. It was an atmosphere that would result in guests returning.

All of this may seem a small thing. However, those in leadership understand how difficult it is to achieve this atmosphere in an enterprise. In the Shangri-La Hotel in Dalian, China, I experienced a level of quality and caring unmatched by any other hotel in my decades of travel. Why? Because the people working there were happy. They were truly valued by their leaders at the hotel, and this directly affected their responses to guests. The leaders of this hotel had achieved something I have never seen in any enterprise.

Truly wise leaders value their people and their people know it. Truly wise leaders create healthy, caring environments where everyone has the capacity to thrive and grow and find their full potential. True leaders want this for their people. They understand their people well enough to give them opportunities to develop their natural gifts and talents. In so doing, truly great leaders help their people find happiness. These are truly great leaders. They lead with a rare wisdom.

Epilogue

In closing, I ask again, what kind of leader will you be? Do you want to open windows of possibilities to your teams? Do you want to nurture others as they reach for their full potential? Do you want them to achieve amazing, startling, wonderful things, or just the same old, boring results? If I know you, you want *amazing*. Good for you. If so, then you must purpose to serve them. You must set your mind to inspire and uplift every day in a thousand small ways. You must speak true, stay focused on the mission, and truly care about your people. And you must tell them these things with your words and actions every day. You are the leader.

> *"Every single employee is someone's son or daughter. Like a parent, a leader... is responsible for their precious lives."*
> Simon Sinek[xxxvii]

Hopefully, this book has inspired you to lead with more passion and purpose. Leadership in project management is more than just running with the mechanics of project management. It is about accomplishing remarkable things with people. There is real joy in leading others as they accomplish remarkable, unexpected, and often impossible things. You, as the leader, have an important charge – to lead well. Now is your time to begin that journey. Lead on!

Appendix

What have we got in the project manager's toolbox?

Project Charter
Project Communication Plan
Weekly Project Status Checkpoint
Monthly Status Reporting
Project Requirements Listing
Project Assumptions Listing
Project Constraints Listing
Project Plan and Gnatt Chart
Project Milestones and Deliverables Checklist
Project Logs Workbook
  Project Risk Log
  Project Action Log
  Project Issue Log
  Project Decision Log
  Project Change Log
Project Change Request
Project Change Order
Project Financial Tracking Workbook
  Financial Overview
  Planned vs Actual Costs
  Earned Value Analysis
  Earned Value Progress Chart
  Contingency and Risk Costs
  Change Costs
  Other Costs

Copy of all project related Agreements, Contracts, etc.
(Not in the appendix but should be in your project repository - a copy of all project related Agreements, Contracts, etc.)

The Project Manager's Digital Toolbox is available at:

gettingamazingthingsdone.com

Project Charter

The Project Charter gives formal recognition to the existence of the project, identifying the objective, stakeholders, and authority of the project manager.

Your Amazing Company

Project Charter

Project Name

Date Submitted   Project Manager

*[*this is a fixed document that does not evolve over the life of the project]*

Objectives and Measurable Outcomes

Key Stakeholders and Team Members

Authority of Project Manager

Sponsor Approval

Sponsor Name

Date Approved

Project Name – Name given to the project

Date Submitted – Date of submission

Project Manager – Designated Project Manager

Objectives and Measurable Outcomes – Description of Objectives and Outcomes

Key Stakeholders and Team Members – Identify Key Stakeholders and Team Members

Authority of Project Manager – Describe authority given to project manager

Sponsor Name – Sponsor Name and signature

Date Approved – Date of approval

Project Communication Plan

The Project Communication Plan establishes how we will formally talk to each other.

Communications Plan   *Your Amazing Company*

Project Name [project name]

Date of Origin [date of origin]   **Version Number*** [version number] **on Date** [version date]

Project Manager [project manager name]

Executive Sponsor [project sponsor name]

[*this is a living document that evolves over the life of the project]

Deliverable (what)	Recipient(s) (who)	Method (how)	Frequency (when)	Responsible Party (owner)
Project Charter	Sponsor, key stakeholders	Meeting to review and approve, on-demand at Sharepoint	One-time	Project Manager
Communication Plan	All Stakeholders	Meeting to review and approve, on-demand at Sharepoint	Meet until approval reached	Project Manager
Project Status Meeting				Project Manager
• Daily Standup	Immediate team	15-minute standup discussion	Daily	
• Weekly Checkpoint	All team members, key stakeholders	Team meeting (virtual, on-site) list location info	Weekly	
• Monthly Executive Status	Executive Steering Committee	Executive meeting (virtual, on-site) list location info	Monthly	
Status Meeting Agendas and Minutes	Designated invitees of the meetings and interested stakeholders	Communiques by email 24 hour prior and following meetings, on-demand at Sharepoint as historic record	As per meeting frequency	
Weekly/Monthly Project Status Reporting • Milestones • Schedule/Cost • Changes • RAID Review	Weekly - All team members, key stakeholders	Email, on-demand at Sharepoint	Weekly	Project Manager
	Monthly - Executive Steering Committee	Email, on-demand at Sharepoint	Monthly	
Change Logs	All Stakeholders	Sharepoint	On-Demand	Project Manager
RAID Logs	All Stakeholders	Sharepoint	On-Demand	Project Manager

Sponsor Approval

Sponsor Signature [project sponsor signature]

Date of Sponsor Approval [date of sponsor approval]

I strongly recommend adding specific team member and stakeholder names to this plan. Consider adding additional sections or pages with specific individuals the project has agreed to communicate with. In addition, I recommend that your plan include specific url links, conference room addresses, and conference call phone numbers as appropriate. Seek extreme clarity with your communications.

Project Name – Name given to the project

Original Date – Date of original Communications Plan

Version Number – Version Number of this version

On Date – Date of this version

Project Manager – Name of project manager

Executive Sponsor – Executive Sponsor Name

Sponsor Signature – Signature of approved executive sponsor

Date of Sponsor Approval – Date of approval

Weekly Project Status Checkpoint

The Weekly Status Checkpoint Reporting serves to keep stakeholders, and particularly the team, apprised of project status. It is a weekly opportunity to recast the vision of the project, keeping the team focused on the objective. Two pages in length.

Weekly Status Checkpoint   Your Amazing Company

Project Name: [project name]

Project Manager: [project manager name]

Report Period: [start date of reporting period]   [end date of reporting period]

Meeting Location:

Overall Project Status: RED/YELLOW/GREEN

Status Summary

Objectives This Period

Milestones achieved
Milestones planned but not achieved
Deliverables achieved
Deliverables planned but not achieved
Interlocks

Objectives Planned Next Period

Milestones planned
Deliverables planned
Interlocks

Significant Risks, Issues, Actions, Decisions, and Changes

Milestones and Deliverables Checklist — Your Amazing Company

	Project:	[Project Name]		
	Reporting Date:	19-Jan-2018		

Project Overview

Initiation		1-Jan-2018	1-Feb-2018	
Description of Milestone	Status	Scheduled	Actual	Variance
Work Product: Project Charter	Completed	31-Jan-2018	28-Jan-2018	3
Deliverable: Communications Management Plan	Completed	31-Jan-2018	28-Jan-2018	3
Deliverable: Risk Management Plan	Completed	31-Jan-2018	31-Jan-2018	0
Deliverable: Project Plan (Preliminary)	Completed	31-Jan-2018	31-Jan-2018	0
Work Product: Resource Plan (Preliminary)	Completed	31-Jan-2018	1-Feb-2018	-1
Milestone: Project Launch Complete	Completed	31-Jan-2018	31-Jan-2018	0

Planning		22-Jan-2018	30-Nov-2018	
Description of Milestone	Status	Scheduled	Actual	Variance
Milestone: Preparation for BusReq Gathering Complete	Completed	9-Feb-2018	9-Feb-2018	0
Milestone: BusReq Preliminary Analysis Complete	Waiting Appv	12-Mar-2018	12-Mar-2018	0
Milestone: BusReq Gap Analysis Complete	In Process	18-Apr-2018		89
Deliverable: Gap Analysis	In Process	25-May-2018		125
Deliverable: Requirements Outline	In Process	25-May-2018		125
Milestone: Final Report - Requirements and Gap Analysis Complete	Not Started	25-May-2018		126

Executing		28-May-2018	28-Jan-2018	
Description of Milestone	Status	Scheduled	Actual	Variance
Interlock: Agreement to proceed with Solution enhancements	Not Started	30-May-2018		131
Milestone: Install Hardware and Software Complete	Not Started	28-Jun-2018		160
Milestone: Analyze Business Requirements	Not Started	18-Jun-2018		150
Milestone: Identify Options to Satisfy Business Requirements	Not Started	22-Jun-2018		154
Milestone: Review Options with Users	Not Started	22-Jun-2018		154
Milestone: Create Functional Specifications	Not Started	29-Jun-2018		161
Milestone: Identify Costs and Priorities	Not Started	29-Jun-2018		161
Milestone: Obtain Client Sign-Off	Not Started	31-Jul-2018		193
Milestone: Prepare Project Plan	Not Started	31-Jul-2018		193
Milestone: Confirm Business Requirements Complete	Not Started	31-Jul-2018		193
Milestone: Configure System Complete	Not Started	24-Sep-2018		248
Milestone: Develop System Enhancements Complete	Not Started	26-Oct-2018		280
Milestone: Conduct Unit/Application Testing Complete	Not Started	28-Nov-2018		313
Deliverable: Application set delivered/installed at Client	Not Started	28-Nov-2018		313
Milestone: Conduct Partial Build Complete	Not Started	10-Dec-2018		325
Milestone: Conduct Complete Build Complete	Not Started	14-Dec-2018		329
Milestone: Create/Modify Policies and Procedures Complete	Not Started	4-Dec-2018		319
Milestone: Conduct Integration Testing Complete	Not Started	12-Dec-2018		327
Milestone: Conduct Stress/Volume Testing Complete	Not Started	31-Dec-2018		346
Milestone: Conduct UAT Testing Complete	Not Started	15-Jan-2019		361
Milestone: Conduct Training Complete	Not Started	10-Dec-2018		325
Milestone: Conduct Go-Live Decision Complete	Not Started	23-Jan-2019		369
Milestone: Go-Live Complete	Not Started	28-Jan-2019		374

Monitoring and Controlling		1-Jan-2018	4-Jan-2019	
Description of Milestone	Status	Scheduled	Actual	Variance
Deliverable: Project Plan	In Process	4-Jan-2019		350
Work Product: Resource Plan	In Process	4-Jan-2019		350

Closing		31-Jan-2019	1-Feb-2018	
Description of Milestone	Status	Scheduled	Actual	Variance
Milestone: Project Execution Complete	Not Started	4-Jan-2019		350
Interlock: New functionality available	Not Started	4-Jan-2019		350

Not Started >	26	67%
In Process >	5	13%
Waiting Appv >	1	3%
Completed >	7	18%
	39	100%

158

Monthly Status Reporting

The Monthly Status Reporting serves to keep stakeholders, and particularly the leadership, apprised of project status. It is a monthly, formal record of the project progress, and to recap the project's benefit to the organization. Four pages in length.

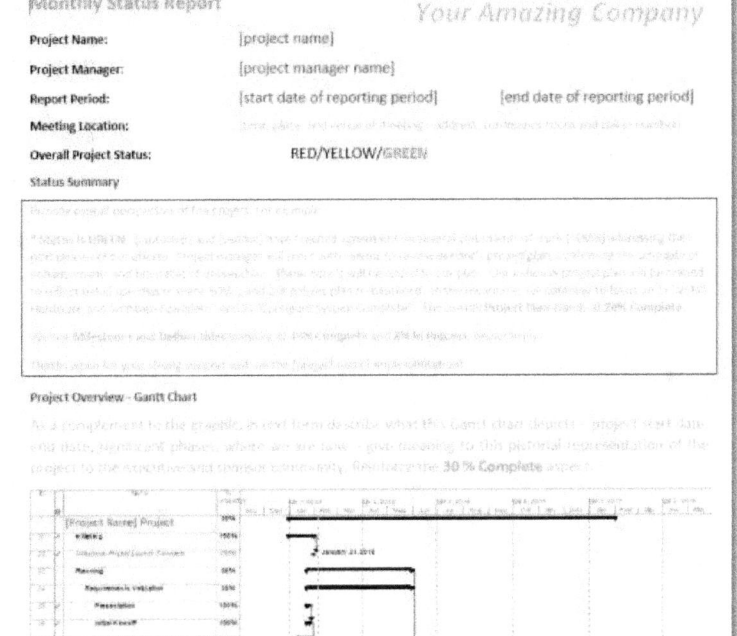

Objectives This Period

Milestones achieved
Milestone: Project Launch Complete

Milestones planned but not achieved
None planned

Deliverables achieved
Deliverable: Communications Management Plan
Deliverable: Risk Management Plan
Deliverable: Project Plan (Preliminary)
Work Product: Resource Plan (Preliminary)
Work Product: Business Gap Analysis Complete

Deliverables planned but not achieved
None planned

Interlocks
None planned

Objectives Planned Next Period

Milestones planned
Milestone: Business Gap Analysis Complete
Milestone: Final Report – Requirements and Gap Analysis Complete

Deliverables planned
Deliverable: Requirements Outline

Interlocks
Interlock: Agreement to proceed with Solution Enhancement

Financial Overview

Budget (BAC):	1,000,000
Percent Complete:	
Planned Value (PV) of Resources:	125,000
Actual Cost (AC) of Resources:	113,000

This cut/paste from Financial Overview page of Financial Tracking spreadsheet gives current standing of the project. Use this area of the status report to elaborate on the project from a numbers perspective. As necessary, restate percent complete and give an overall sense of the state of the project.

Earned Value:	index
Schedule Performance Index (SPI)	0.85
Cost Performance Index (CPI)	0.70
To Complete Performance Index (TCPI)	1.04
Calculated Earned Value (EV)	80,000

Earned Value appreciation begins here and continues on subsequent page. Here you are giving the executives and sponsors the basic information. On the follow-on page, you will give them the back up data and pictorial chart.

Burn Rate:	1.44

Talk about burn rate. A value of 1.00 is right on the mark. Values less than 1 indicate we are burning resources at less than expected rates. Values greater than 1 indicate that we are burning resources more quickly than expected.

Summary of Project Costs:	planned	actual
Cost of Resources	124,500	113,000
Contingency Reserve	100,000	0
Cost of Risk	3,684	0
Cost of Change	0	5,750
Other Costs	0	10,215
Total Costs »	227,484	130,965
Project Cost Overrun/Underrun »	96,719	

This provides a simple recap of each category of expense. Elaborate for any categories showing unexpected change.

Overrun/Underrun is a simple indicator of what remains in the project budget.

Earned Value Analysis

In text form describe what is happening with Earned Value. This classic Earned Value Analysis (EVA) chart depicts progressive movement of Actual Cost and Earned Value against Planned Value. Ideally, Actual Cost and Earned Value move around the Planned Value throughout the life of the project. Deviation of Earned Value away from Planned Value for two periods is an indicator of problems on the project. This pictorial representation of the project serves as a call to action for the executive and sponsor community.

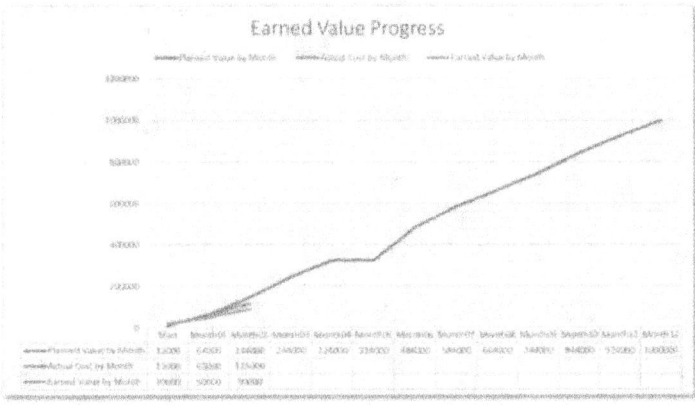

Earned Value Progress

Earned Value Indicators ('000s)							
PV	AC	EV	SV	CV	SPI	CPI	TCPI
148	115	90	-58	-25	0.83	0.78	1.05

PV = Planned Value = BCWS = Budgeted Cost of Work Scheduled
AC = Actual Cost = ACWP = Actual Cost of Work Performed
EV = Earned Value = BCWP = Budgeted Cost of Work Performed
TCPI = To Complete Performance Index

CV = Cost Variance
SV = Schedule Variance
CPI = Cost Performance Index
SPI = Schedule Performance Index

Significant Risks, Issues, Actions, Decisions, and Changes

Highlight significant risks and issues. This is also the place to highlight all risks, issues, actions, decisions, and changes. This is where you highlight only items that may have a significant impact. For example –
- Risk 1 short description here.
- Risk 2 short description here.
- Issue 1 short description here.
- Issue 2 short description here.

Milestones and Deliverables Checklist — *Your Amazing Company*

| | | Project: | [Project Name] | |
| | | Reporting Date: | 12-Mar-2018 | *Reporting date must be equal to or greater than a Milestone Date in line* |

Project Overview		1-Jan-2018	1-Feb-2018	
Initiating		1-Jan-2018	1-Feb-2018	
Description of Milestone	Status	Scheduled	Actual	Variance
Work Product: Project Charter	Completed	31-Jan-2018	28-Jan-2018	3
Deliverable: Communications Management Plan	Completed	31-Jan-2018	28-Jan-2018	3
Deliverable: Risk Management Plan	Completed	31-Jan-2018	31-Jan-2018	0
Deliverable: Project Plan (Preliminary)	Completed	31-Jan-2018	31-Jan-2018	0
Work Product: Resource Plan (Preliminary)	Completed	31-Jan-2018	1-Feb-2018	-1
Milestone: Project Launch Complete	Completed	31-Jan-2018	31-Jan-2018	0

Planning		22-Jan-2018	30-May-2018	
Description of Milestone	Status	Scheduled	Actual	Variance
Milestone: Preparation for BusReq Gathering Complete	Completed	9-Feb-2018	8-Feb-2018	1
Work Product: BusReq Preliminary Analysis Complete	Completed	12-Mar-2018	12-Mar-2018	0
Milestone: BusReq Gap Analysis Complete	Waiting Appv	18-Apr-2018		37
Deliverable: Gap Analysis	In Process	25-May-2018		74
Deliverable: Requirements Outline	In Process	25-May-2018		74
Milestone: Final Report - Requirements and Gap Analysis Complete	Not Started	25-May-2018		74

Executing		30-May-2018	28-Jan-2019	
Description of Milestone	Status	Scheduled	Actual	Variance
Interlock: Agreement to proceed with Solution enhancements	Not Started	30-May-2018		79
Milestone: Install Hardware and Software Complete	Not Started	28-Jun-2018		108
Milestone: Analyze Business Requirements	Not Started	18-Jun-2018		98
Milestone: Identify Options to Satisfy Business Requirements	Not Started	22-Jun-2018		102
Milestone: Review Options with Users	Not Started	22-Jun-2018		102
Milestone: Create Functional Specifications	Not Started	29-Jun-2018		109
Milestone: Identify Costs and Priorities	Not Started	29-Jun-2018		109
Milestone: Obtain Client Sign-Off	Not Started	31-Jul-2018		141
Milestone: Prepare Project Plan	Not Started	31-Jul-2018		141
Milestone: Confirm Business Requirements Complete	Not Started	31-Jul-2018		141
Milestone: Configure System Complete	Not Started	24-Sep-2018		196
Milestone: Develop System Enhancements Complete	Not Started	26-Oct-2018		228
Milestone: Conduct Unit/Application Testing Complete	Not Started	28-Nov-2018		261
Deliverable: Application set delivered/installed at Client	Not Started	28-Nov-2018		261
Milestone: Conduct Partial Build Complete	Not Started	10-Dec-2018		273
Milestone: Conduct Complete Build Complete	Not Started	14-Dec-2018		277
Milestone: Create/Modify Policies and Procedures Complete	Not Started	4-Dec-2018		267
Milestone: Conduct Integration Testing Complete	Not Started	12-Dec-2018		275
Milestone: Conduct Stress/Volume Testing Complete	Not Started	31-Dec-2018		294
Milestone: Conduct UAT Testing Complete	Not Started	15-Jan-2019		309
Milestone: Conduct Training Complete	Not Started	10-Dec-2018		273
Milestone: Conduct Go-Live Decision Complete	Not Started	23-Jan-2019		317
Milestone: Go-Live Complete	Not Started	28-Jan-2019		322

Monitoring and Controlling		1-Jan-2019	4-Jan-2019	
Description of Milestone	Status	Scheduled	Actual	Variance
Deliverable: Project Plan	In Process	4-Jan-2019		298
Work Product: Resource Plan	In Process	4-Jan-2019		298

Closing		31-Jan-2019	1-Feb-2019	
Description of Milestone	Status	Scheduled	Actual	Variance
Milestone: Project Execution Complete	Not Started	4-Jan-2019		298
Interlock: New functionality availabe	Not Started	4-Jan-2019		298

Not Started >	26	67%
In Process >	4	10%
Waiting Appv >	1	3%
Completed >	8	21%
	39	100%

Project Requirements Listing

The Project Requirements Listing that I recommend is a simple spreadsheet format with three tabs defined as 1) the Requirements, 2) Assumptions, and 3) Constraints. Add other details as your situation may demand.

Here is the Requirements Listing.

ID – Unique identifying number for requirement

Description of Requirement – Description of requirement

Submitted By – Person submitting requirement

Date Submitted – Date of submission

Owner – Person who follows up on requirement

Status –

blank - no decision

In Scope - requirement is in scope of project

Deferred - requirement is out of scope for project - retain details for future effort

Rejected - requirement is out of scope for project

Additional Comment or Reference – Additional comments or references including rationale for accept or reject if necessary

Project Assumptions Listing

The Project Requirements Listing that I recommend is a simple spreadsheet format with three tabs defined as 1) the Requirements, 2) Assumptions, and 3) Constraints. Add other details as your situation may demand.

Here is the Assumptions Listing.

ID – Unique identifying number for assumption

Description of Requirement – Description of assumption

Submitted By – Person submitting assumption

Date Submitted – Date of submission

Owner – Person who follows up on assumption

Status –

blank - no decision - by default, assumption is accepted without comment

Accepted - assumption is accepted as a limiting boundary for project

Rejected - assumption is rejected as a limiting boundary for project

Additional Comment or Reference – Additional comments or references including rationale for accept or reject if necessary

Project Constraints Listing

The Project Requirements Listing that I recommend is a simple spreadsheet format with three tabs defined as 1) the Requirements, 2) Assumptions, and 3) Constraints. Add other details as your situation may demand.

Here is the Constraints Listing.

Constraints Listing			[Project Name]	[date]	Your Amazing Company		
ID	Description of Constraint		Submitted by	Date Submitted	Owner	Status	Additional comment or reference
1							
2						Status:	
3						blank - no decision - by default, constraint is accepted without comment	
4						Accepted - constraint is accepted as a limiting boundary for project	
5						Rejected - constraint is rejected as a limiting boundary for project	
6							
7							
8							
9							
10							
11							
12							
13							
14							
15							
16							
17							
18							
19							
20							

ID – Unique identifying number for constraint

Description of Requirement – Description of constraint

Submitted By – Person submitting constraint

Date Submitted – Date of submission

Owner – Person who follows up on constraint

Status –

> blank - no decision - by default, constraint is accepted without comment

> Accepted - constraint is accepted as a limiting boundary for project

> Rejected - constraint is rejected as a limiting boundary for project

Additional Comment or Reference – Additional comments or references including rationale for accept or reject if necessary

Project Plan with Gantt Chart

Here we see a typical project plan with Gantt view, employing the five standard project processes of initiating, planning, executing, monitoring and controlling, and closing. In order to capture the essence of the view, I have closed or compressed much of the detail (note the *twisties* along the left edge). I recommend including a view like this in the Monthly Status Report to give an overview of the progress of the project. Using such images also communicates that there are logical tools and a specific framework supporting the project effort. This helps to build the confidence of our leadership, providing them a rationale to champion our efforts.

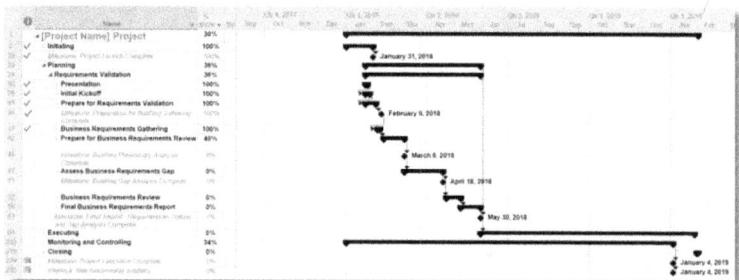

Next, we see an alternative project plan with Gantt view employing a Six Sigma approach of define, measure, analyze, improve, control. Whether a traditional standard approach or Six Sigma, or some other structured framework, I recommend including a high-level Gnatt view of the project in the Monthly Status Report, providing a window into our project methodology to build support for our approach.

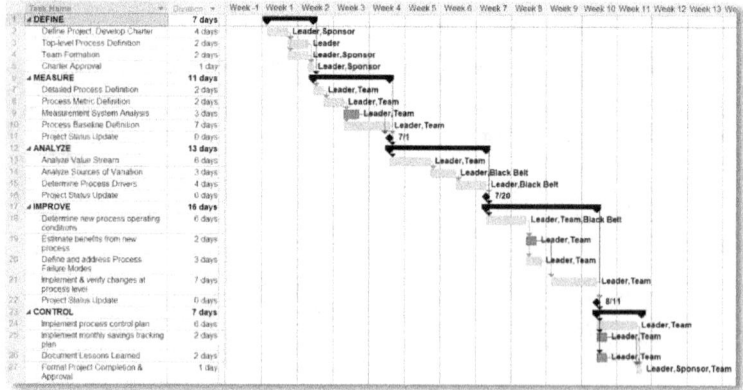

166

Project Milestones and Deliverables Checklist

		Project:	[Project Name]		
		Reporting Date:	########		

Project Overview			1-Jan-2018	1-Feb-2019	
Initiating			1-Jan-2018	1-Feb-2018	
Description of Milestone	Status	Scheduled	Actual	Variance	
Work Product: Project Charter	Completed	31-Jan-2018	28-Jan-2018	3	
Deliverable: Communications Management Plan	Completed	31-Jan-2019	28-Jan-2018	3	
Deliverable: Risk Management Plan	Completed	31-Jan-2018	31-Jan-2018	0	
Deliverable: Project Plan (Preliminary)	Completed	31-Jan-2018	31-Jan-2018	0	
Work Product: Resource Plan (Preliminary)	Completed	31-Jan-2018	1-Feb-2018	-1	
Milestone: Project Launch Complete	Completed	31-Jan-2018	31-Jan-2018	0	

Planning			########	########	
Description of Milestone	Status	Scheduled	Actual	Variance	
Milestone: Preparation for BusReq Gathering Complete	Completed	9-Feb-2018	8-Feb-2018	1	
Work Product: BusReq Preliminary Analysis Complete	Completed	12-Mar-2018	12-Mar-2018	0	
Milestone: BusReq Gap Analysis Complete	Waiting Appv	18-Apr-2018		37	
Deliverable: Gap Analysis	In Process	25-May-2018		74	
Deliverable: Requirements Outline	In Process	25-May-2018		74	
Milestone: Final Report - Requirements and Gap Analysis	Not Started	25-May-2018		74	

Executing			########	########	
Description of Milestone	Status	Scheduled	Actual	Variance	
Interlock: Agreement to proceed with Solution enhancements	Not Started	30-May-2018		79	
Milestone: Install Hardware and Software Complete	Not Started	28-Jun-2018		108	
Milestone: Analyze Business Requirements	Not Started	18-Jun-2018		98	
Milestone: Identify Options to Satisfy Business Requirements	Not Started	22-Jun-2018		102	
Milestone: Review Options with Users	Not Started	22-Jun-2018		102	
Milestone: Create Functional Specifications	Not Started	29-Jun-2018		109	
Milestone: Identify Costs and Priorities	Not Started	29-Jun-2018		109	
Milestone: Obtain Client Sign-Off	Not Started	31-Jul-2018		141	
Milestone: Prepare Project Plan	Not Started	31-Jul-2018		141	
Milestone: Confirm Business Requirements Complete	Not Started	31-Jul-2018		141	
Milestone: Configure System Complete	Not Started	24-Sep-2018		196	
Milestone: Develop System Enhancements Complete	Not Started	26-Oct-2018		228	
Milestone: Conduct Unit/Application Testing Complete	Not Started	28-Nov-2018		261	
Deliverable: Application set delivered/installed at Client	Not Started	28-Nov-2018		261	
Milestone: Conduct Partial Build Complete	Not Started	10-Dec-2018		273	
Milestone: Conduct Complete Build Complete	Not Started	14-Dec-2018		277	
Milestone: Create/Modify Policies and Procedures Complete	Not Started	4-Dec-2018		267	
Milestone: Conduct Integration Testing Complete	Not Started	12-Dec-2018		275	
Milestone: Conduct Stress/Volume Testing Complete	Not Started	31-Dec-2018		294	
Milestone: Conduct UAT Testing Complete	Not Started	15-Jan-2019		309	
Milestone: Conduct Training Complete	Not Started	10-Dec-2018		273	
Milestone: Conduct Go-Live Decision Complete	Not Started	23-Jan-2019		317	
Milestone: Go-Live Complete	Not Started	28-Jan-2019		322	

Monitoring and Controlling			1-Jan-2018	4-Jan-2019	
Description of Milestone	Status	Scheduled	Actual	Variance	
Deliverable: Project Plan	In Process	4-Jan-2019		298	
Work Product: Resource Plan	In Process	4-Jan-2019		298	

Closing			########	1-Feb-2019	
Description of Milestone	Status	Scheduled	Actual	Variance	
Milestone: Project Execution Complete	Not Started	4-Jan-2019		298	
Interlock: New functionality available	Not Started	4-Jan-2019		298	

Not Started >	26	67%
In Process >	4	10%
Waiting Appv >	1	3%
Completed >	8	21%
	39	100%

The Milestones and Deliverables Checklist is an important tool in your toolbox. This simple tool helps you keep the team highly focused on key progress markers. So, how do we build and maintain it throughout the project duration?

The Project Milestones and Deliverables Checklist is a simple spreadsheet format. It is based on the detailed task lines in the project plan. Once the project plan has been developed and approved, certain elements of the project plan are captured into the Project Milestones and Deliverables Checklist. The checklist begins with two values:

Project – Name of the project

Reporting Date – This is the period ending date for the current reporting period. The value used here *impacts number of days calculations* in the checklist.

Here I need to elaborate on technique that I have used over the years that is used to create the checkpoint. Within MS Project and other similar tools, milestones are designated using a flag in the task line detail within MS Project. It is worth noting that a milestone has no duration or resources. This means that they have no impact on the cost or schedule; they are simply points in time along the project continuum. Think of them as simply markers or checkpoints. In my work I use the designation of *milestone* for several things – milestones, work products, deliverables, and inter-locks. Why? This keeps these key aspects active in the project plan and visible to all. Any time we are looking at the plan, our eyes are reminded of these key signposts.

For clarity, let me define each of these four things.

Milestone – A significant event or achievement accomplished on the project
Work Product – A significant output from the team that *is not* designated in the project scope or contractual agreements, produced for the convenience of the team
Deliverable – An output from the team that *is* designated in the project scope or contractual agreements, produced for the benefit of the sponsor or client
Interlock – A critical point-in-time interface with an entity outside the project, where the project may impact, or be impacted by the other, a point-in-time awareness

In addition, I capture them into the checkpoint spreadsheet we are currently exploring, and this becomes a central communication element on the project. How do I use the milestone designation? First, the task line must be flagged as a milestone within MS Project. Second, the task description is *keyed in a particular way* to aid the reader in understanding the nature of that line. Here are examples of each use:

Milestone: Analyze Business Requirements
Work Product: Resource Plan
Deliverable: Requirements Outline
Interlock: New Functionality Available for Fall Trade Show

As we see, whether a line is a milestone, work product, deliverable, or interlock is clear to the reader. Now, let's return to the Project Milestones and Deliverables Checklist.

As we said, designated milestones (including milestones, work products, deliverables, and interlocks) are captured into the spreadsheet. I like to create categories representing the five project life cycles stages – initiating, planning, executing, monitoring and controlling, and closing. Within these groupings, we capture the related designated milestones. (as in the foregoing example) Each designated milestone row includes the following values:

Description of Milestone – A description of the designated milestone beginning with the following format *[designated milestone type]:*

Status – Status of milestone as follows:

   Not Started – Designated milestone has not begun
   In Process – Designated milestone has begun and is in process
   Waiting Appv – Designated milestone is completed and awaiting final approval
   Completed – Designated milestone is complete and approved

Scheduled – Scheduled date for completion

Actual – Actual date of completion, blank indicates not completed

Variance – Days variance between scheduled and actual completion dates

If completed with actual date:

   – positive value (+) indicates number of days ahead of schedule when achieved

   - negative value (-) indicates number of days behind schedule when achieved

   - zero value indicates that designated milestone achieved as planned

If not complete and actual date is blank, then reporting date is used to calculate number of days until designated milestone is scheduled to be completed - how soon before it is due

Project Logs Workbook

The Project Logs Workbook that I recommend is a simple spreadsheet format with five tabs defined as 1) the Project Risk Log, 2) Project Action Log, 3) Project Issue Log, 4) Project Decision Log, and 5) Project Change Log. Often referred to as the RAID logs. The following pages detail each log.

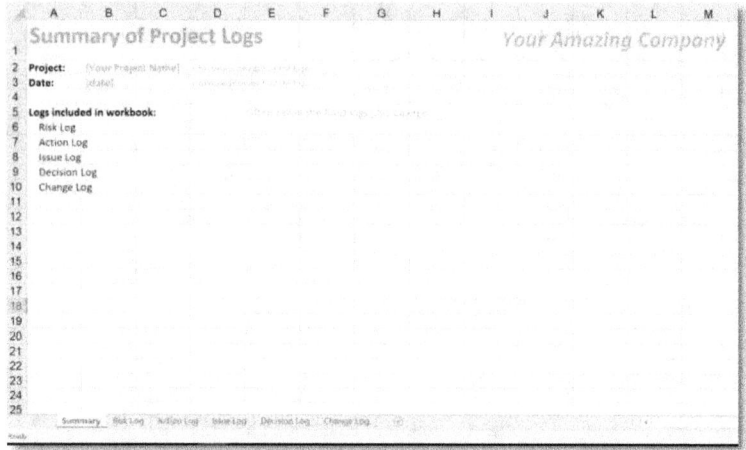

Project Logs Workbook

    Project Risk Log

    Project Action Log

    Project Issue Log

    Project Decision Log

    Project Change Log

Project Risk Log

The Project Risk Log includes the following cells. Add others as your situation may demand.

Risk Log		[Your Project Name]		[date]			Your Amazing Company			
ID	Short Description	P	Probability	Impact	Severity/Exposure	Date Raised	Raised By	Owner	Target Date	St	Status Date	Comment
1					0							
2					0							
3					0							
4					0							
5					0							
6					0							
7					0							
8					0							
9					0							
10					0							
11					0							
12					0							
13					0							
14					0							
15					0							
16					0							
17					0							
18					0							
19					0							
20					0							

ID – Unique identifying number for risk

Short Description – Short description of risk

P – Priority of risk as H-High, M-Medium, or L-Low

Probability – Probability that risk will incur expressed as 1.0 for low, 2.0 for medium, 3.0 for high

Impact – Impact that risk will incur expressed as 1.0 for low, 2.0 for medium, 3.0 for high

Severity/Exposure – Product of Probability and Impact (P*I) should risk occur

Date Raised – Date that risk was raised and logged

Raised By – Person identifying risk

Owner – Person who follows up on risk

Target Date – Targeted date of risk resolution or dissolution

St – Status of risk as O–Open, C–Closed, or R-Rejected

Status Date – Date of must current status update

Comment – Additional comments

Project Action Log

The Project Action Log includes the following cells. Add others as your situation may demand.

Action Log		[Your Project Name]			[date]		Your Amazing Company		
ID	Short Description	P	Owner	Date Assigned	Target Date	Date Launched	Date Performed/Completed	St	Associated action IDs	Comment
1										
2										
3										
4										
5										
6										
7										
8										
9										
10										
11										
12										
13										
14										
15										
16										
17										
18										
19										
20										

ID – Unique identifying number for action

Short Description – Short description of action

P – Priority of action as H-High, M-Medium, or L-Low

Owner – Person who follows up on action

Date Assigned – Date of action assigned to owner

Target Date – Targeted date of action completion

Date Launched – Date action began

Date Performed/Completed – Date action was performed or completed

St – Status of action as O–Open, A-Assigned, or C–Closed

Associated action IDs – IDs of any related actions

Comment – Additional comments

Project Issue Log

The Project Issue Log includes the following cells. Add others as your situation may demand.

Issue Log		[Your Project Name]	[date]	Your Amazing Company						
ID	Short Description	P	Issue Consequences	Date Raised	Raised By	Owner	Target Date	St	Status Date	comment
1										
2										
3										
4										
5										
6										
7										
8										
9										
10										
11										
12										
13										
14										
15										
16										
17										
18										
19										
20										

ID – Unique identifying number for issue

Short Description – Short description of issue

P – Priority of action as H-High, M-Medium, or L-Low

Issue Consequences – Anticipated outcomes of this issue

Date Raised – Date issue was raised and logged

Raised By – Person who raised the issue

Owner – Person who follows up on risk

Target Date – Targeted date of risk resolution or dissolution

St – Status of action as O–Open, C–Closed, or R-Rejected

Status Date – Date of most current status update

Comment – Additional comments

Project Decision Log

The Project Decision Log includes the following cells. Add others as your situation may demand.

Decision Log		[Your Project Name]			[date]		Your Amazing Company		
ID	Short Description	P	Notable Impacts of Decision		Date Raised	Raised By	Decision Date	St	Status Date	comment

ID – Unique identifying number for decision

Short Description – Short description of decision

P – Priority of action as H-High, M-Medium, or L-Low

Notable Impacts of Decision – Noteworthy impacts of this decision

Date Raised – Date decision was raised and logged

Raised By – Person who raised the decision

Decision Date – Date a decision is needed

St – Status of decision as blank-Under Discussion, C-Decision Complete

Status Date – Date of most current status update

Comment – Additional comments

Project Change Log

The Project Change Log includes the following cells. Add others as your situation may demand.

ID – Unique identifying number for change

Short Description – Short description of change

P – Priority of action as H-High, M-Medium, or L-Low

Change Outcomes – Anticipated outcomes from the change

Date Submitted – Date change submitted for consideration

Submitted By – Person submitting change

Analysis Approval – Date of analysis approval

Analysis Completed – Date analysis of change completed

CO Submitted – Date Change Order submitted

CO Complete – Date Change Order completed

St – Status of change request as follows:

Submitted - Change Request submitted
Analysis - Change Request is being evaluated
Approved - Change Request has been approved
Deferred - Change Request has been deferred to future
Rejected - Change Request has been rejected
Scheduled - Change Order has been created/scheduled
Completed - Change Order has been implemented

Status Date – Date of most current status update

Comment – Additional comments

Project Change Request

The Project Change Request that I recommend tracks the progress of a Change Request from inception through approval of initial estimate, to an analysis of the change, and subsequent approval or not, and movement to Change Order status if needed.

Change Request

Your Amazing Company

Project Name:	[project name]
Project Manager:	[project manager name]
Change Request Number:	[change request number]
Date of Change Request Submission:	[change request submission date]

Description of Change

Anticipated Outcomes of Change

Estimated Cost of Analyzing Change Request	[estimated cost of analyzing change]
Decision on Change Request Analysis	[approved/deferral/rejection]
Date of Change Request Analysis Decision	[date of change request analysis decision]
Change Request Analysis Decision by	[person signing change request analysis decision]

Summary Findings of Change Request Analysis

Estimated Impact of Change Request to Scope, Cost, and Schedule

Decision on Change Request	[approved/deferral/rejection]
Date of Change Request Decision	[date of change request decision]
Change Request Decision by	[person signing change request decision]
Date of Change Order Created	[date of change order created/scheduled]
Date of Change Order Completion	[date of change order completion/implementation]

Project Name – Name of project

Project Manager – Name of project manager

Change Request Number – Unique identifying number for change

Date of Change Request Submission – Date change submitted for consideration

Description of Change – Description of change

Anticipated Outcomes of Change – Description of anticipated outcomes, benefits to the enterprise, rationale to accept the change

Estimated Cost of Analyzing Change Request – The cost, or hours required to review and estimate this Change Request

Decision on Change Request Analysis – Decision to proceed with analyzing the Change Request is Accept, Defer, or Reject

Date of Change Request Analysis Decision – Date of CR analysis decision

Change Request Analysis Decision By – Person making analysis decision

Summary Finding of Change Request Analysis – Description of summary findings of analyzing the Change Request

Estimated Impact of Change Request to Scope, Cost and Schedule – Impact of Change Request on the project baselines of Scope, Cost, and Schedule

Decision on Change Request – Decision to proceed with analyzing the Change Request is Accept, Defer, or Reject

Date Change Order Created – Date of Change Order created

Date of Change Order Completed – Date of Change Order completed

Project Change Order

The Project Change Order that I recommend tracks the progress of a Change Order from receipt out of Change Request process through implementation and approval.

Change Order		Your Amazing Company
Project Name:	[project name]	
Project Manager:	[project manager name]	
Change Order Number:	[change order number]	
Date of Change Created/Scheduled:	[change order created date]	
Description of Change Order		

[large blank box]

Realized Impact of Change Order to Scope, Cost, and Schedule

[blank box]

Date of Change Order Completion	[date of change order completion/implementation]
Change Order Completion by	[person signing change order completion/implementation]

Project Name – Name of project

Project Manager – Name of project manager

Change Order Number – Unique identifying number for change order

Date of Change Order Submission – Date change order created or scheduled

Description of Change Order – Description of change

Realized Impact of Change Order to Scope, Cost, and Schedule– Description of actual, realized impact to project baselines of scope cost, and schedule

Date of Change Order Completion – Date of Change Order completed

Change Order Completion By – Person making analysis decision

Project Financial Tracking Workbook

The Project Financial Tracking Workbook that I recommend is a simple spreadsheet format with five tabs with seven components defined as 1) the Financial Overview, 2) Planned vs Actual Costs, 3) Earned Value Analysis, 4) Earned Value Progress Chart, 5) Contingency and Risk Costs, 6) Change Costs, 7) Other Costs. The following pages detail each component.

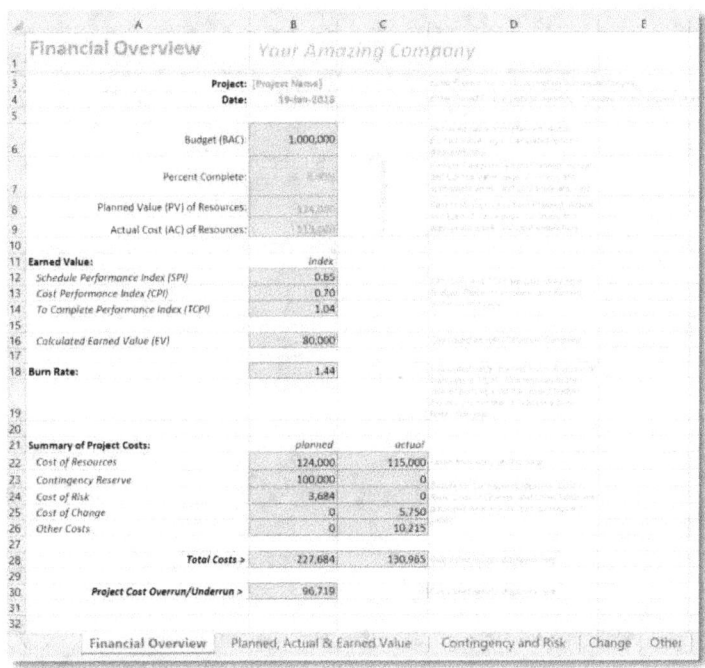

Project Financial Tracking Workbook

Financial Overview

Planned vs Actual Costs

Earned Value Analysis

Earned Value Progress Chart

Contingency and Risk

Change Costs

Other Costs

Financial Overview

The Financial Overview tab includes the following cells. Add others as your situation may demand.

Financial Overview	Your Amazing Company		
Project:	[Project Name]		
Date:	19-Jan-2018		
Budget (BAC):	1,000,000		
Percent Complete:	8.00%		
Planned Value (PV) of Resources:	124,000		
Actual Cost (AC) of Resources:	115,000		
Earned Value:	*index*		
Schedule Performance Index (SPI)	0.65		
Cost Performance Index (CPI)	0.70		
To Complete Performance Index (TCPI)	1.04		
Calculated Earned Value (EV)	80,000		
Burn Rate:	1.44		
Summary of Project Costs:	*planned*	*actual*	
Cost of Resources	124,000	115,000	
Contingency Reserve	100,000	0	
Cost of Risk	3,684	0	
Cost of Change	0	5,750	
Other Costs	0	10,215	
Total Costs >	227,684	130,965	
Project Cost Overrun/Underrun >	96,719		

Project – Name of project – this entered value will populate other project name value on subsequent tabs

Date – Current reporting date – this entered value is typically set to next reporting date – it populates project reporting date on subsequent tabs

Budget (BAC) – Budget at Completion – this value is retrieved from Planned, Actual, Earned Value tab with calculated results displayed here

Percent Complete – Percent Complete – the value for current period is found on Planned, Actual, Earned Value tab and posted here

Planned Value (PV) of Resources – Planned Value for current period is found on Planned, Actual, Earned Value tab and posted here

Actual Cost (AC) of Resources – Actual Cost for current period is found on Planned, Actual, Earned Value tab and posted here

Schedule Performance Index (SPI) – SPI is calculated from BAC, Percent Complete, and Earned Value (EV) on this tab

Cost Performance Index (CPI) – CPI is calculated from BAC, Percent Complete, and Earned Value (EV) on this tab

To Complete Performance Index (TCPI) – TCPI is calculated from BAC, Percent Complete, and Earned Value (EV) on this tab

Calculated Earned Value (EV) – EV is calculated as BAC * Percent Complete

Burn Rate – This is a calculated value. Earned Value Analysis of burn rate is 1/CPI

Schedule Performance Index (SPI) – SPI is calculated from BAC, Percent Complete, and Earned Value (EV) on this tab

Cost of Resources – Cost of resources planned and actual are taken from PV and AC entered on this tab

Contingency Reserve – This value is retrieved from Contingency, Risk, Change tab

Cost of Risk – This value is retrieved from Contingency, Risk, Change tab

Cost of Change – This value is retrieved from Contingency, Risk, Change tab

Other Costs – This value is retrieved from Other Costs tab

Total Costs – This is a calculated sum of planned and actual costs

Project Cost Overrun/Underrun – This is a calculated value of the project's net position at this time

Planned vs Actual Costs

The Planned vs Actual, Earned Value tab includes the following cells for tracking Planned vs Actual Costs. Add others as your situation may demand.

Planned, Actual and Earned Value   [Project Name]   19-Jan-2018

Blended Hourly Rate	100

Planned vs Actual

Planned Hours

	Planned Cost	Week 1	Week 2	Week 3	Week 4	Week 5	Week 6
Resource 1	208000	40	40	40	40	40	40
Resource 2	208000	40	40	40	40	40	40
Resource 3	204000	40	40	40	40	40	40
Resource 4	192000			40	40	40	40
Resource 5	188000			40	40	40	40
Total Planned (PV)	1000000	120	120	200	200	200	200
Cumulative Planned Hours>	10000	120	240	440	640	840	1040

Actual Hours

	Actual Cost	Week 1	Week 2	Week 3	Week 4	Week 5	Week 6
Resource 1	28000	40	40	40	40	40	40
Resource 2	28000	40	40	40	40	40	40
Resource 3	25000	30	40	20	40	40	40
Resource 4	22000		40	20	40	40	40
Resource 5	12000			40	40		40
Total Actual (AC)	115000	110	160	160	200	160	200
Cumulative Actual Hours>	1150	110	270	430	630	790	990

Project Name – Retrieved from Financial Overview tab

Project Reporting Date – Retrieved from Financial Overview tab

Blended Hourly Rate – The value entered here drives the overall cost of project resources

Planned Hours – The table for planned hours provides for establishing anticipated use of individual resources by week throughout the duration of the project – once established and agreed to by stakeholders, this table represents the project baseline and should not be altered except in the event of a substantial agreed-to change – these values are the basis of earned value calculations

Planned Cost – The Planned Hours table is summed for each resource adjacent to represents total cost for each resource

Total Planned – The Planned Hours table totals all planned resource cost – this is total planned value, or Budget at Completion

Actual Hours – The table for actual hours provides for entering, week-by-week, actual resource hours throughout the duration of the project - these values are the basis of earned value calculations

Actual Cost – The Actual Hours table is summed for each resource adjacent to the resource name – this represents actual cost to date for each resource

Total Actual – The Actual Hours table totals all actual resource cost – this is total actual resource cost to date on the project

182

Earned Value Analysis

The Planned vs Actual, Earned Value tab includes the following cells for tracking Earned Value Analysis (EVA). Add others as your situation may demand.

Earned Value Analysis

	Week 1	Week 2	Week 3	Week 4	Week 5	Week 6
Percent Complete>	2.00%	3.00%	4.00%	5.00%	6.00%	7.00%
	Week 1	Week 2	Week 3	Week 4	Week 5	Week 6
Planned Value	12000	24000	44000	64000	84000	104000
Actual Cost	11000	27000	43000	63000	79000	99000
Earned value	20000	30000	40000	50000	60000	70000
Schedule Variance Position	20000	30000	40000	50000	60000	70000
Cost Variance Position	21000	27000	41000	51000	65000	75000
	Week 1	Week 2	Week 3	Week 4	Week 5	Week 6
Schedule Performance Index	1.67	1.25	0.91	0.78	0.71	0.67
Cost Performance Index	1.82	1.11	0.93	0.79	0.76	0.71
To Complete Performance Index	0.99	1.00	1.00	1.01	1.02	1.03
Schedule Variance	8000.00	6000.00	-4000.00	-14000.00	-24000.00	-34000.00
Cost Variance	9000.00	3000.00	-3000.00	-13000.00	-19000.00	-29000.00
	Week 1	Week 2	Week 3	Week 4	Week 5	Week 6
	Month01				Month02	

Percent Complete – Percent complete is derived from project plan – typically Microsoft Project or other tools – and posted each week – this percentage drives the other Earned Value Measurement (EVM) calculations

Planned Value – This embedded calculation is based planned hours table for the current period and blended rate - the value for the current period is entered into the Financial Overview tab

Actual Cost – This embedded calculation is based on actual hours table for the current period and blended rate - the value for the current period is entered into the Financial Overview tab

Earned Value – This embedded calculation is based on total planned (BAC) in the planned hours table and percent complete for current period

Schedule Variance Position – This calculated value is available if you want to add a track for Schedule Variance on the Earned Value Chart

Cost Variance Position – This calculated value is available if you want to add a track for Cost Variance on the Earned Value Chart

Schedule Performance Index – SPI is calculated EV/PV for each weekly period

Cost Performance Index – CPI is calculated EV/AC for each weekly period

To Complete Performance Index – TCPI is calculated (BAC-EV)/(BAC/AC) for each weekly period

Schedule Variance – SV is calculated EV-PV for each weekly period

Cost Variance – CV is calculated EV-AC for each weekly period

Earned Value Progress Chart

The Planned vs Actual, Earned Value tab includes the following for displaying Earned Value Analysis (EVA). This is the classic Earned Value Analysis chart.

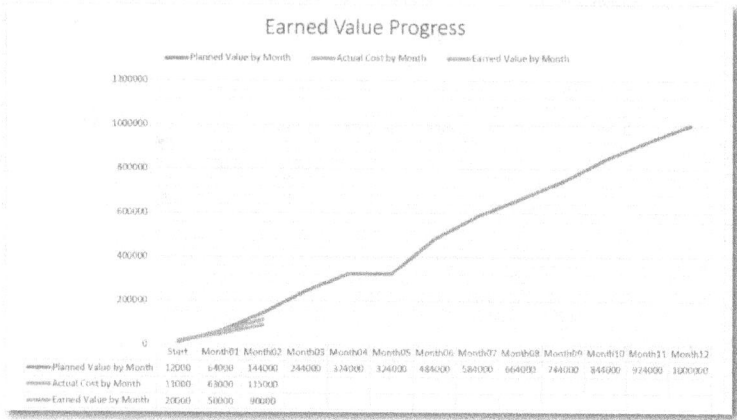

Earned Value Progress Chart – This graph displays the week-by-week progress of the project from an Earned Value perspective. At the outset of the project – once the planned hours have been entered – the planned value line is shown from project inception to completion – as the project advances by the week, the actual cost and earned value appear.

The Earned Value Analysis Chart is displayed here for periodic review and analysis. In addition, I recommend using cut/paste to include it into Weekly Status Checkpoint and Monthly Status Reporting with accompanying text explanation of results including SPI, CPI, and TCPI indices analysis. Using EVM tools the teams become familiar with EVM analysis, and easily use them to monitor their own and overall team performance. This is one aspect of keeping the team focused on the mission.

184

Contingency and Risk Costs

The Contingency and Risk tab includes the following cells for tracking contingency and risk costs. Add others as your situation may demand.

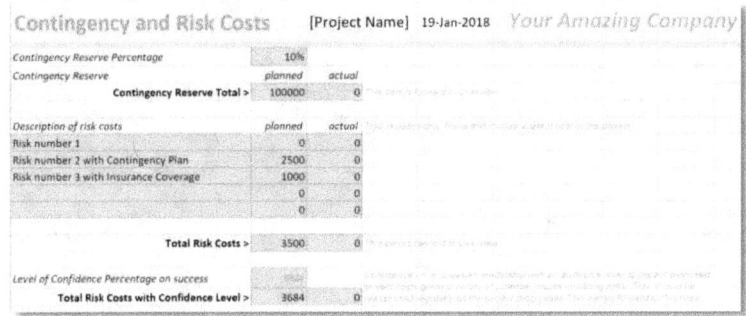

Project Name – Retrieved from Financial Overview tab

Project Reporting Date – Retrieved from Financial Overview tab

Contingency Reserve Percentage – The value entered here drives contingency reserve amount – this value is often dictated by organizational guidelines

Contingency Reserve – Planned is calculated value of Total Planned (PV) from Planned vs Actual, Earned Value tab and Contingency Reserve Percentage – Actual is an entered value of contingency funds that have been applied to project

Risk Costs – Planned risk costs are the cost of risks having a likelihood of realization especially if those costs are substantial - actual risk costs are entered values of realized risks that have resulted in added costs to the project

Total Risk Cost – The sum of all planned and actual risk costs

Level of Confidence Percentage on Success – The level of confidence that leadership has regarding the success of the project stated as a percentage likelihood of success

Total Risk Costs with Confidence Level – The total risk cost is adjusted by confidence level yielding a refined risk total which accounts for the confidence level

185

Change Costs

The Change tab includes the following cells for tracking change costs. Add others as your situation may demand.

Change Costs	[Project Name]		######### Your Amazing Company
Description of change costs	planned	actual chg request id	additional description of change costs
Change 1	0	3000	Modification to scope to include new web feature
Change 2	0	2750	Modification in scope to include additional stakehold need
Total Project Change Costs >	0	5750	

Project Name – Retrieved from Financial Overview tab

Project Reporting Date – Retrieved from Financial Overview tab

Description of Change Costs – Short description of change request

Planned Change Costs – Planned change costs are the cost of change having a likelihood of realization, especially if those costs are substantial - actual change costs are entered values of approved changes that have resulted in added costs to the project

Actual Change Costs – Actual change costs are the cost of change that have been approved and have resulted in added costs to the project

Chg Request ID – Identifying number of Change Request that this cost reflects

Additional Description of Change Costs – Additional description as necessary

Total Project Change Costs – Planned and Actual total change costs is a sum of the detailed costs

186

Other Costs

The Other Costs tab includes the following cells for tracking other costs. Add others as your situation may demand.

Other Project Costs	[Project Name]		19-Jan-2018	Your Amazing Company
Description of other costs	planned	actual	additional description of other costs	
Additional Software 1	0	1500	Additional software tool needed in development	
Additional Software 2	0	975	Software for testers	
Additional Software 3	0	2345	Additional software to upgrade key development tool	
Added Celebratory Event 1	0	3295	Event to reward team for accomplishing Milestone 2 ahead of schedule	
Added Celebratory Event 2	0	2100	Event to reward team for accomplishing Milestone 5 ahead of schedule	
Total Project Other Costs >	0	10215		

Project Name – Retrieved from Financial Overview tab

Project Reporting Date – Retrieved from Financial Overview tab

Description of Other Costs – The short description of other costs

Planned – Anticipated other costs to the project

Actual – Actual other cost incurred by the project

Additional Description of Other Costs – Additional description as necessary

Total Project Other Costs – Planned and Actual total other costs is a sum of the detailed costs

Earned Value Formulas

Earned Value Analysis involves a number of formulas. In my own work, some of these formulas are embedded in my Project Financial Tracking Workbook on the tab involving earned value calculations. Here I include a list of the basic formulas used for the convenience of the reader. Keep in mind that project management theorists are always elaborating on these basic formulaic structures, adding nuanced changes.

This information from PMBOK® 6th Edition pages 261-267.[xxxviii]

EARNED VALUE FORMULAS				
Abbv	Name	Definition	Equation	Interpretation
PV	Planned Value	Authorized budget assigned to scheduled work as of a point		
AC	Actual Cost	Realized cost incurred for work		
EV	Earned Value	Measure of work performed expressed in terms of budget authorized for that work at a point in time	EV = sum of planned value of completed work (Formula for entire	
BAC	Budget at Completion	Project budget or total planned value, sometimes		
CV	Cost Variance	Measure of cost performance, amount by budget deficit or surplus at a point in time	CV = EV - AC	Positive = Under planned cost Neutral = On planned cost Negative = Over planned cost
SV	Schedule Variance	Measure of schedule performance, amount by which project is ahead or	SV = EV - PV	Positive = Ahead of schedule Neutral = On schedule Negative = Behind schedule
VAC	Variance at Completion	Estimated difference in cost at completion of project	VAC = BAC - EAC	Positive = Under planned cost Neutral = On planned cost Negative = Over planned cost
CPI	Cost Performance Index	Measure of cost efficiency expressed as a ration between EV and AC at a point in time	CPI = EV/AC	Greater than 1.0 = under planned cost Exactly 1.0 = On planned cost Less than 1.0 Over planned cost
SPI	Schedule Performance Index	Measure of schedule efficiency expressed as a ratio between EV to PV at a point in time	SPI = EV/PV	Greater than 1.0 = ahead of schedule Exactly 1.0 = On schedule Less than 1.0 Behind schedule
EAC	Estimate at Complete	Estimated total cost at completion at a point in time	1) EAC = BAC/CPI 2) EAC = AC + BAC - EV	1) If CPI is expected to be the same for remainder of the project 2) future work will be accomplished at planned rate (other calculations from PMI if other situations exist
ETC	Estimate to Complete	Estimated cost going forward to complete the project from a	BAC - AC	Assuming work is proceeding on plan
TCPI	To Complete Performance	Measure of cost performance that must be achieved with remaining resources in order	TCPI = (BAC - EV) / (BAC - AC)	Greater than 1.0 = Harder to complete Exactly 1.0 = Same to complete Less than 1.0 Easier to complete

Index

Acknowledgements

Somewhere along the way I stumbled into a wonderful thing. People can achieve objectives way beyond what we may have thought possible. People have the capacity to take us to places we have only just glimpsed in a dream, to places beyond even our own imagination. I have worked with teams of people facing impossible requirements and budgets and schedules, things not doable according to the plans. And I have seen those teams vastly exceed expectations to deliver amazing results. How was it possible? Somewhere along the way I noticed that people could do amazing things if the leader created a nurturing climate where incredible outcomes could incubate and grow into something truly wonderful.

I am deeply indebted to all the people and teams that I have had the honor to serve over the years. They have taught me so much I cannot measure it. It exceeds mind and heart. I can only say thank you. It has been my joy.

My family has ever been my most ardent supporters. My wife Robbie, the love of my life, has always been my closest companion and friend, encouraging me to share these ideas. My children, Abbey, Ethan, and Seth, having endured my many years of relentless travel, and they have often asked me to "tell of tale", knowing that others would find these things inspiring and perhaps life-changing. And they were right. Lives have changed. I am much indebted to each of them and profoundly blessed with their love and sacrifice, and their patience and understanding. It is beyond words.

Robbie and Abbey also helped with the initial editing.

I must also thank many colleagues from around the world that offered to review the manuscript, providing helpful guidance and encouragement. I owe them much for their thoughtfulness and willingness to take the time to read the book and provide their valued insights. These friends include:

Fran Bado, Executive Project Manager, IBM (Retired), US Virginia

Michael Coleman, PM Learning Program Manager, IBM, United Kingdom

Ben Cox, Senior Director, Viewpoint Construction Software, US Oregon

Jamin Dick, PMP, former SVP Global Supply Chain, Pitney Bowes, US New York

Raymond Price, Vice President of Business Development, DiscoverX Corporation, US California

Tadeu Veiga, PMP, Management and Professional Development Consultant, TadeuV8, Brazil

Padmanaban Venkataramanan, PMP, Leader PM Curriculum, IBM India (Retired), India

Thomas Walenta, PgMP, PMP, PMI Fellow, Germany

And there are others. To everyone who has encouraged me to share my leadership ideas, this book is for you. Time to go out and lead with true passion and joy.

Bibliography

DePree, M. (1992). *Leadership Jazz.* New York: Doubleday, a division of Bantam Doubleday Dell Publishing Group, Inc.

DePree, M. (2004). *Leadership is an Art.* New York: Crown Publishing Group, a division of Random House LLC, Penguin Random House Company.

Katzenbach, J. R., & Smith, D. K. (1993). *The Wisdom of Teams.* New York: Harvard Business School Press.

Kouzes, J. M., & Posner, B. Z. (2002). *Leadership Challenge Third edition.* San Francisco, CA: Jossey-Bass Company.

PMI-PMBOK-5thEd. (2013). *PMBOK® Guide 5th Edition.* Newtown Square, PA: Project Management Institute, Inc.

PMI-PMBOK-6thEd. (2017). *PMBOK® Guide 6th Edition.* Newtown Square, PA: Project Management Institute, Inc.

Pyzdek, T., & Keller, P. (2014). *The Six Sigma Handbook 4th Edition.* New York: McGraw Hill Education.

Sinek, S. (2009). *Start with Why.* New York: Penguin Group.

Sinek, S. (2014). *Leaders Eat Last.* New York: Penguin Group.

Sproul, R. C. (2005). *The Reformation Study Bible English Standard Version.* Lake Mary, Florida: Ligonier Ministries.

E n d n o t e s

[i] (DePree, 2004) 11

[ii] (Sinek, 2014) 83

[iii] (Kouzes and Posner, 2002) 152

[iv] (PMI-PMBOK-6thEd, 2017) 716

[v] (PMI-PMBOK-6thEd, 2017) 33

[vi] (Katzenbach and Smith, 1993) 91

[vii] (Katzenbach and Smith, 1993) 91

[viii] (Katzenbach and Smith, 1993) 91

[ix] (Katzenbach and Smith, 1993) 92

[x] (Katzenbach and Smith, 1993) 92

[xi] (PMI-PMBOK-6thEd, 2017) 18

[xii] (PMI-PMBOK-6thEd, 2017) 40

[xiii] (PMI-PMBOK-6thEd, 2017) 19

[xiv] (PMI-PMBOK-6thEd, 2017) 189-190

[xv] (PMI-PMBOK-6thEd, 2017) 711

[xvi] (PMI-PMBOK-6thEd, 2017) 704

[xvii] (PMI-PMBOK-6thEd, 2017) 707

[xviii] (PMI-PMBOK-6thEd, 2017) 725

[xix] (PMI-PMBOK-6thEd, 2017) 720

[xx] (PMI-PMBOK-6thEd, 2017) 395

[xxi] (PMI-PMBOK-5thEd, 2013) 544

[xxii] (PMI-PMBOK-5thEd, 2013) 122

[xxiii] (PMI-PMBOK-6thEd, 2017) 261

[xxiv] (PMI-PMBOK-5thEd, 2013), 218.

[xxv] (PMI-PMBOK-5thEd, 2013) 219

[xxvi] (PMI-PMBOK-5thEd, 2013) 218

[xxvii] (PMI-PMBOK-5thEd, 2013) 219

[xxviii] (PMI-PMBOK-5thEd, 2013) 221

[xxix] (PMI-PMBOK-6thEd, 2017) 553

[xxx] (PMI-PMBOK-6thEd, 2017) 675

[xxxi] (PMI-PMBOK-5thEd, 2013) 229

[xxxii] (Pyzdek and Keller, 2014) 4

[xxxiii] (Pyzdek and Keller, 2014) 4

[xxxiv] (PMI-PMBOK-5thEd, 2013) 236-238

[xxxv] http://www.quotationspage.com/quote/26950.html

xxxvi (Sproul, 2005) 607
xxxvii (Sinek, 2014) 19
xxxviii (PMI-PMBOK-6thEd, 2017) 261-267

About the Author

Henry Lewis traveled the world for ten years with IBM conducting classes and workshops to project managers and leaders. In his years as principal of a software development consulting firm and an executive project manager with IBM, he led numerous successful engagements across many industries. His expertise in handling troubled projects helped otherwise failing projects, pull back from the brink, and finish with extraordinary results. Henry will tell you the teams were amazing.

Henry consults in project management and leadership, working with companies and their people to achieve amazing outcomes. He thrives on helping others find their voice as leaders, as they reach high and lead others to stunning solutions.

Henry lives in the Minneapolis area where he writes, works, plays, and purposes to help others lead with contagious joy believing for amazing, startling, and wonderful things.

About the Book

This book was borne out of a desire to inspire others to lead with passion and commitment to the mission and the people. There is a pure joy in leading others well. This book attempts to guide us as we lead others to accomplish amazing, startling, and wonderful things.

If you would like additional copies of the book, information on workshops, and other helpful resources, please visit our website at:

gettingamazingthingsdone.com

www.ingramcontent.com/pod-product-compliance
Lightning Source LLC
Chambersburg PA
CBHW051309220526
45468CB00004B/1272